Loneliness

as a Way of Life

Loneliness

as a Way of Life

THOMAS DUMM

HARVARD UNIVERSITY PRESS

Cambridge, Massachusetts

London, England

2008

A Caravan book. For more information, visit *www.caravanbooks.org*

Library of Congress Cataloging-in-Publication Data
Dumm, Thomas L.
Loneliness as a way of life / Thomas Dumm.
p.   cm.
Includes bibliographical references and index.
ISBN-13: 978-0-674-03113-5 (alk. paper)
1. Political science—Philosophy.   2. Loneliness.   3. Grief.   I. Title.

JA66.D84 2008
320.01—dc22   2008006567

To William E. Connolly

Contents

Preface

Why would someone who has devoted so much of his adult life to the study of politics write a book about loneliness? Isn't it a radical departure from the concerns of polity to focus on a subject that on the face of it has nothing to do with our political condition? Does it even matter for our politics whether we are lonely?

I believe that it matters profoundly. *Loneliness as a Way of Life* is the result of a lengthy and sometimes convoluted intellectual and emotional journey, but the core intuition that has persistently informed the thinking and the writing of this book is that many of our most important understandings about the shape of our present communal existence—the division between public and private, our inability to live with each other honestly and in comity, the estranged and isolating forms that our relationships with our most intimate acquaintances sometimes assume, the weakness of our attachments to each other and hence to our lives in common—are all manifestations of the loneliness that has permeated the modern world.

We are the inheritors of a legacy of loneliness. But loneliness is not something that can easily be described through the usual ways of doing political theory. As I worked on this book, it gradually became clear to me that the subject of loneliness, because of its isolating qualities—what I call "the experience of the pathos of disappearance"—is resistant to understanding by means of the ordinary tools of description, critique, and analysis. Instead, I realized that I would need to supplement those tools in order to explore and understand the powerful influence that loneliness has on modern life. So as this book unfolds, its tone and substance become increasingly personal. In retrospect, it appears that I may have written something akin to a mystery story, one that concerns itself not only with the emergence of a modern form of loneliness, but with its ongoing presence as a common experience in our time. To illuminate this presence, in the end I had no recourse other than to supplement my study of the loneliness of others with an ongoing study of my own lonely self.

You who read this book will need to judge whether it meets a particular test, whether the way I have described loneliness rings true. But the terms and conditions of your assessment will require a different set of criteria than is usual for books that take on such a subject. I ask that you try to bring as much of yourself to this book in response to what I have tried to bring to it. Descend to meet me, if you will.

I am grateful to the John Simon Guggenheim Foundation for awarding me a fellowship for the 2001–2002 academic year. That fellowship, supplemented by the generous support of the Board of Trustees at Amherst College in the form of sabbatical support for two leaves and a senior faculty research award, enabled me to take the time to think through this project and to rethink and rewrite it as experience and circumstance demanded.

Collegial encouragement in the form of invitations to speak on the subject of loneliness also helped me think through this project. At Penn State University, Johns Hopkins University, Connecticut College, Bard College, and Simon's Rock of Bard College, I was treated with generosity and kindness. I thank Nancy Love, William Connolly, Jane Bennett, Jennifer Culbert, Richard Flathman, David Kyuman Kim, Julie Rifkin, Thomas Keenan, Ann Lauterbach, Norton Batkin, and Asma Abbas for their hospitality on these occasions. Russell Goodman invited me to Santa Fe to teach at the National Endowment for the Humanities Summer Institute on "Emerson at 200" in the summer of 2003. Russell and Stephen Affeldt, the assistant director of the project, enabled me to think through a series of issues concerning Emerson, individuality, and loneliness. On all these occasions, the members of the audience were remarkably attentive and engaged by what I had to say. To the extent that any of you whom I met during these encounters hear your own voice in this book, please take it as a hopeful sign that I heeded your words and learned from them. I am thankful for your small mercies.

I am also grateful for the continued support of friends and colleagues over the period of the writing of this book. In Amherst town, Julian Olf, a writer friend who is also a professor of theater at the University of Massachusetts, read my musing on *Lear* at an important moment. Another dear friend, Jennifer Michelson, read much of the penultimate draft of this book and offered the perspective of an acutely intuitive nonacademic thinker. More generally, the denizens of Rao's Coffee shared the everyday with me as I wrote in their presence. Among other good friends, Heidi Stemple read the manuscript in full, offering trenchant editorial advice with the practiced eye of a professional writer.

I also wish to thank my Amherst College colleagues Kim Townsend, Nasser Hussain, and Austin Sarat for their ongoing engagement with my work. My colleagues at the *Massachusetts Review* have been patient with me as I neglected my duties there to finish this project, but they also have done more, publishing a small piece of it. Let David Lensen stand for all in my acknowledgment of their aid. Chip Turner, Wendy Brown, Mort Schoolman, Kennan Ferguson, Andrew Norris, Lisa Disch, Kitty Holland, Anne Norton, Jane Bennett, Peter Rush, Cornel West, Alison Young, Bob Gooding-Williams, Larry George, Elizabeth Young, Carolin Emcke, Ted Lowi, Michael Shapiro, Linda Garman, Bill Chaloupka,

Alex Hooke, and Ted Plimpton all may find some of their alienated thoughts returning to them here.

This is the first book I have worked on with Lindsay Waters of Harvard University Press. Lindsay insisted that I find my own voice, and as a result the book is now both shorter and more direct, much better than it was when it first came to him. He also suggested the title at a key moment, leading me to finally and fully realize that this is in fact the subject of the book—a way of life.

My brother John Dumm, my sister Catherine Doherty, and my daughter Irene Bright-Dumm read much of the manuscript of this book and shared their own perceptive knowledge about the familial circumstances that are the subject of some of its contents. I am profoundly grateful to them.

There are three friends of long standing whose presence I always find when I write. Ann Lauterbach's amazing poetry has inspired my less successful prose. Her passionate commitment to language— its way of expressing our states of being and becoming—continually instructs me in the heartening economy of metaphor. Stanley Cavell's impact on my understanding of philosophical matters should be readily apparent to anyone who has read his work. My wonder about where his words end and mine begin might be labeled the anxiety of influence, except that I feel less anxious and more happy when he is present in my present. That he allows me to be his friend is a source of deep gratitude. Finally, Bill Connolly, my interlocutor for decades now, has done more to encourage me than I deserve. I dedicate this book to him as a small acknowledgment of his many kindnesses over the years.

Elements of several of the chapters of this book have appeared in other forms in previous publications, and I am grateful to the publishers for their permission to reuse this material. Parts of the Prologue appeared as "Cordelia's Calculus: Love and Loneliness in

Cavell's Reading of *Lear*," in *The Claim to Community: Essays on Stanley Cavell and Political Philosophy*, ed. Andrew Norris (Stanford: Stanford University Press, 2006), 212–235. The several pages of Chapter 2 that address the identity of Pip and Ishmael appeared in the September 2005 issue of the *Massachusetts Review* as "Who Is Ishmael?" Finally, the discussion of Du Bois and Emerson in Chapter 4 appeared in another form as "Political Theory for Losers" in *Vocations in Political Theory*, ed. Jason Frank and John Tambernino (Minneapolis: University of Minnesota Press, 2001), 145–165.

Prologue

Cordelia's Calculus

Her father the King has just announced that he is abdicating. Her sisters have avidly praised the old man, swearing their love in absolute terms in order to get their shares of his estate. Now he turns to the youngest daughter to elicit her testimony of love in front of the assembled court. Somehow we already feel that the kingdom hangs in the balance with her response.

The right words of love and she inherits her share. If she fails to say the right words, bad things will happen. That her sisters cannot be trusted is proven by the answers they have just provided, answers so fulsome as to reveal their falseness. Partly because of their claims of love, Cordelia cannot bring herself to say what her father wants her to say. It isn't that she doesn't love him. But it is also not possible for her to say what she feels without it feeling false to her.

Why does *she* feel a sense of falseness? After all, she isn't like her sisters, professing a love they do not feel in order to inherit. What is the matter with Cordelia? Why is she stuck? And why is her father demanding this testimony? As sovereign, Lear is above all other mortals in this kingdom, but from the moment of abdication he will fall to a place where he will have nothing—no power, no assurance of recognition, not even a shelter from the storm. And yet he

abdicates anyway, gives up his power without reckoning the consequences. Why does he do it? It has a lot to do with the fact that he
loves his daughters. They are his final connection to this earth; they
are his only line to whatever future he may still aspire to. But there
is something more at work than a father's love here, even his love in
opposition to the demands of sovereign responsibility. Out of Lear's
love for his daughters grows a profound sorrow, a recognition that
they have suffered something awful already in their lives, a suffering
which he cannot repair, but which deepens his desire to give them
something, everything he can give, as a compensation for their
loss.

Shakespeare's *Tragedy of King Lear* long ago assumed mythic status, insinuating itself into the dreams of all of us. Harold Bloom
has gone so far as to claim that in his plays and poems Shakespeare
actually invented what it means to be human, and if anything *Lear*
is Shakespeare's most fully human play. Although what matters the
most in the tale has been told and retold, the heart of its hurt is not
so easily expressed. What may be most important about this play
has everything to do with an as yet—always as yet—unarticulated
feeling of loss. This tragedy is a story of losses, nothing but. A kingdom is riven, a king goes mad, a family is destroyed, a good man is
blinded, many die, and the very idea of love itself is made to appear
as a folly. How does all this happen?

There is, of course, Lear himself. He is a monster of a man, enormous of soul, large enough to go to war with the world, and large
enough to go to war with himself as well. When he becomes mad—
driven mad, we usually say, but by whom?—we can see how fear-
some he is, his psychic powers unchecked and unraveling. Here he
is out in the storm, refusing shelter, hoping that the distraction will
keep him from his evil-dwelling thoughts about the older daughters
who have so grievously insulted him after he gave them his estate.
His struggle is somatic, his body revolting against his soul.

Lear. Thou think'st 'tis much that this contentious storm
Invades us to the skin; so 'tis to thee;
But where the greater malady is fix'd,
The lesser is scarce felt. Thou'dst shun a bear,
But if [thy] flight lay toward the roaring sea,
Thou'dst meet the bear i' th' mouth. When the mind's free,
The body's delicate; [this] tempest in my mind
Doth from my senses take all feeling else,
Save what beats there—filial ingratitude!
Is it not as this mouth should tear this hand
For lifting food to't? But I will punish home.
No, I will weep no more. In such a night
To shut me out? Pour on, I will endure.
In such a night as this? O Regan, Goneril!
Your old kind father, whose frank heart gave all—
O, that way madness lies, let me shun that!
No more of that.

(III.iv.6–22)[1]

Lear's mouth and hand are like his daughters and himself: his body can withstand the storm from the heavens but not the storm from his brain and his gut, the storm that began with his abdication, the rage that he projects upon his children. His raging mind is overwhelming his delicate body. It is taking from his senses all feeling, voiding the contents of his body, concentrating the very beat of his heart on the powerful and obsessively throbbing, painful idea—the constant thought of the refusal of his two well-dowered daughters to shelter him. He struggles with that mind through his body, but he is rent by the struggle.

A Cartesian split between body and mind is enacted here on a mighty scale. That split is a fact of life for sovereign beings, well described in the medieval doctrine of the King's Two Bodies, in which God's chosen sovereign is said to possess both a mortal and an immortal body. Lear's immortal body is escaping into the storm, while his mortal body is exposed to the elements, cracked wide open. He becomes more human than any of us, brought into a shape and scale both familiar and yet shocking. We see the mighty man in his diminished state, and he remains a man. But even as he rages honestly, and suffers with a clarity that communicates a great power, he still is lying—if only to himself—about what makes his heart beat this way, because while he gave all his goods to Regan and Goneril, his heart was not true in the giving. Had it been so, he would not have expected a return of even false love from them. So Lear goes into the storm to escape from himself, his shame, the horror of his own bad behavior, giving his earthly possessions to those who falsely loved him, exiling the one daughter who did love him. He goes to the frontier to get away from the settlements of his divided kingdom. But he cannot get away from himself. To do that he must go mad, and even that is not enough in the end.

What is the character of this rage that follows in the train of his shame? In thinking about his descent into madness and his recovery (such as it is), a key to comprehending Lear's character is the fact that this man is, after all, a king attempting to give up not only his material possessions but his sovereign power as well. Abdication puts Lear in an impossible position in regard to filial devotion—he wants to give his children everything, but because he is sovereign he must demand proof of their love in return, he must *dictate* the terms of his abdication. Hence, he would be happiest if in response to his demand for love he were to receive, not authentic statements, but counterfeit expressions. Then he could at least comfort himself with not having to know *truly* whether his daughters love him. When Cordelia fails to comply with his demand, she reveals the emptiness behind it. Lear is ashamed to want the expression of freely given love, having always dictated the terms by which he would be loved. This exposure of his shame sets the tragedy in motion. Out of his shame, Lear becomes enraged, first at Cordelia for being true and later at Goneril and Regan for being truly false. Their true falseness is revealed when they reject him from their homes, which means that they are sending him into exile, expelling him from the kingdom that he had bequeathed to them as a result of having divided his own. (And yet this exile is incomplete, for he still wanders through the kingdom, exposed to the elements, but not cast out.) We might be tempted to say that while on the throne Lear had wanted false love, but now that he is off the throne he wants true love, if only he could find it.

But is love ever truly true? Can we find in the divisions of kingdom and love, of love and loss, of divided love and wounded selves, anything that resembles the truth of love? Goneril and Regan give their father false love while he rules in return for power upon his abdication, but now that they have power, why shouldn't they see his request for shelter as offensive, as a renewed demand for the counterfeit expression they only gave him when he held sovereign power over them? Niceties of etiquette aside, Lear can only represent a threat to them now, and so they will deal with him accordingly. Their calculus is straightforward: do unto Lear before he does unto them. And Cordelia? We will need to reckon with her love, measure how close she comes to true love, and how far away.

So to the storm. Having imagined himself rejected by Goneril, upon his departure from her castle Lear sends ahead his servant, the disguised Kent, to announce his untimely visit to his other favored daughter, Regan. Arriving at Regan's castle, he comes upon his unfortunate emissary in stocks, a result of the fact that Goneril had sent her servant Oswald to warn Regan of Lear's coming. When he learns of Kent's harsh treatment at the hands of Regan, Lear is outraged. In a moment of transcendent anger he warns himself of the madness welling up within him:

Lear. O how this mother swells up toward my heart!
[*Hysterica*] *passio,* down thou climbing sorrow,
Thy element's below.—Where is this daughter?
(II.iv.56–58)

This exclamation is the first overt acknowledgment by Lear of his madness. It is an extraordinary moment in which the various themes of the play find expression—love, loss, (mis)recognition, shame, sovereignty, and nihilism, all circling around one word— "mother." The *Riverside Shakespeare* comments on this passage that "mother" means hysteria, which connects it to the Greek *husterikos*—of the womb. Tracing the word "mother" through the *Oxford English Dictionary,* we observe a metonymic chain of associated meanings at work in a series of definitions that emerge in the late fourteenth century. In one definition "mother" is defined as the womb—and this part of the body serves to define the whole body. When the womb becomes disordered, then the word describes the disorder of "*a rising (suffocation, swelling upward) of the mother. Hysteria.*"[2]

The hysteria of the mother plays a crucial role in the madness of Lear, linking his bodily condition to the deepest metaphorical powers available to him. Imagination becomes embodied through a series of gender displacements. There is a silent doubling at the heart of this tragedy, in which Lear's abdication—the loss of the Crown that ultimately results in the loss of the King himself—is paralleled by an offstage tragedy in which the loss of the Queen, the mother (a loss that may have triggered the abdication in the first place), results in the loss of the Queen's daughter, Cordelia. (Cordelia is the most likely to be this Queen's daughter, since she is the youngest of the three children. And we may be permitted to wonder if that same Queen is the mother of Regan and Goneril, if somehow these broken ties of blood and birth are inscribed in the very frame of this tragedy.)

Love and loss—where *is* the mother in *Lear?* We will again and again circle back to this beginning, to the crucial moment of abdication which sets these events in motion. We do not know why Lear chooses this moment, of all moments, to abdicate. In the universe of the play, his decision to abdicate occurs offstage, a silent prologue to the first act. Misrecognition and shame—is Lear himself somehow trying to be the mother of these motherless children, and is this a source of his shame? If Lear's hysteria is an expression of his impossible wish to mother his children, this may explain his desire to receive only their signs of love, not the real thing. For he is ill-equipped to receive the love that children may have for their mother.

The moment of what may be Lear's most repulsive expression of hate lends credence to this idea. When Lear, still mad, meets Gloucester immediately after the latter is led by Edgar to the false edge of the Dover cliff, Lear responds when the blinded man recognizes his voice.

> *Lear.* Ay, every inch a king!
> When I do stare, see how the subject quakes.
> I pardon that man's life. What was thy cause?
> Adultery?
> Thou shall not die. Die for adultery? No,
> the wren goes to't, and the small gilded fly
> Does lecher in my sight.
> Let copulation thrive; for Gloucester's bastard son
> Was kinder to his father than my daughters
> Got 'tween the lawful sheets.
> To't, luxury, pell-mell, for I lack soldiers.
> Behold, yond simp'ring dame,
> Whose face between her forks presages snow;
> That minces virtue, and does shake the head
> To hear of pleasure's name—

The fitchew nor the soiled horse goes to't
With a more riotous appetite.
Down from the waist they are Centaurs,
Though women all above;
But to the girdle do the gods inherit,
Beneath is all the fiends': there's hell, there's darkness,
There is the sulphorous pit, burning, scalding,
Stench, consumption. Fie, fie, fie! pah, pah!
Give me an ounce of civet, good apothecary,
Sweeten my imagination. There's money for thee.

(IV.vi.107–131)

Lear's kingly consideration of the pardonable adulterer places these matters in terrible context: there is no other way to read this passage than as a vision of women's sexuality as an expression of great evil, Bosch-like in its hellish festering. Lear makes an oblique yet overwhelming comparison to the evil of that fruit of illegitimate if not adulterous love, that bastard son of Gloucester—Edmund, he who bears responsibility both for his father's blinding and for Cordelia's death. Lear begins his tirade by suggesting that women are to be considered as animals below the waist, but he then goes on to say, using the Elizabethan slang for women's genitalia, "hell," that there is a fiendish corruption emitted from their bodies that is beyond the merely animal, something deeply, fetidly, rottenly evil. And it is a torment for Lear to think that from his lawful sheets, from his wife's evil bit, came his daughters. In this rant, it all comes together as a misogyny that reduces, if not completely eliminates, distinctions, most importantly the distinction that might be made between love and mere lust.

How is Lear to overcome this mad hatred? It may be that the deepest pathos of this most misogynistic passage is expressed in the line "Sweeten my imagination"—that in this terrifying speech Lear is expressing much more than a hatred of women, that his misog-

yny is a cover for his fearful rage against mortality itself, the complex interplay of life and death, the very harm of living. Who could
be more acutely aware of the harm of mortality than the King, he
who bears immortality in his office? In the very next lines Lear, in
response to Gloucester's request to kiss his hand, responds, "Let me
wipe it first, it smells of mortality" (IV.vi.133). Lear seeks to overcome his stench, a stench of death, but given his just-completed
and ferocious meditation on the genitalia of women, we may also
imagine that he is referring to the stench of birth as well. This inter-
twining of life and death in the context of sovereign being is a
representation of the worst sort of catastrophe that can befall us,
a trauma so deep as to lead us into the temptation to give up on
life itself for not being worth the pain. And yet it is in the face of
such catastrophe that we actually become more fully who we are
to be.

In his important essay on Lear, "The Avoidance of Love," Stanley Cavell has suggested that Shakespeare hopes to represent Lear's
self-understanding that love itself is inherently debased, precisely
because given his sovereign power he cannot know whether he is
loved or not. For Lear, the thought of this debased love "is a mad-
dening thought; but still more comforting than the truth. For some
spirits, to be loved knowing you cannot return that love, is the most
radical of psychic tortures."[3] This debased love cannot be expressed
beyond the relation of one's embodied self to the world one inhabits, and yet Lear's duty is somehow to be beyond this world. It may
be that his deepest love is his love of the dead mother, and this love
is beyond this world as well.

His horror is that of the father who has failed, because he cannot
mother his motherless children. It is too much for him, precisely
because to allow the mother to rise up would be to give in to his
own madness. In this way, his madness drives him mad. Lear cannot look at himself, for if he did he would be forced to stare into an
abyss of lovelessness, and this he cannot do. Cast into the storm,

stripped naked, he is close to representing bare life, but it is a life for which he must still provide a matrix in the face of his existence. He must, in a sense, give birth to himself, and because he must provide this birthing out of the mother, he remains ashamed. We may see that debased love as a matrix torn from its moorings, a rising mother. Lear would rather be nothing than be a mother. And yet Lear may be the mother of us all.

This turning inward, this folding in of the self upon itself in the face of the loss of the mother, places us squarely in the world of modernity. At this moment, shame is transformed into guilt. We internalize the sovereign powers that we once could see inscribed on the bodies of kings and queens. Lear begins in shame, and becomes ashamed to admit that he is ashamed. His shame begins with his treatment of Cordelia. Cordelia loves her father. His abdication will be her loss as well, not her gain. But what is it that leads him to abdicate if not the death of the mother? Grief-stricken, the King by his sovereignty is already placed above the constraints of ordinary mortals, but in abdication he risks falling below the threshold of ordinary existence, into a nothingness unlike all others. The struggle he enacts is to be present in the world when he has renounced all claims on those in whose presence he wishes to be. Cordelia offers something else, and Lear's tragedy may be figured as his failure to recognize, not only the fact of her love, but the kind of love she has to offer.

If we imagine that Lear is thinking of the missing mother when he contemplates abdication, then when we turn again to the extraordinary first scene of the play, the scene of abdication, we can see more clearly how Cordelia's pronouncement of her love so moves us. For the missing mother is never more present than when a father is speaking to his daughter about the burdens and pleasures of inheritance. What would the mother have had to say, how would she have mediated between father and daughter, comforting both, showing each a way out of the hole they had dug? We only know that there is nothing she can say now. Cordelia tries to imitate her, but fails.

Cordelia's first words are an aside to herself:

> *Cor.* [*Aside.*] What shall Cordelia speak? Love,
>   and be silent.
>
>   (I.i.62)

Cordelia sees her silence as a way out of a dilemma. So she loves *by being silent.* Her second speech is another aside, a report, not on her impaired ability to speak, but on the ponderousness of her love.

> *Cor.* [*Aside.*] Then poor Cordelia!
>   And yet not so, since I am sure my love's
>   More ponderous than my tongue.
>
>   (I.i.76–78)

Only then does she respond directly to Lear. This is the famous first part of their exchange:

> *Lear.* . . .—Now, our joy,
>   Although last and least, to whose young love
>   The vines of France and milk of Burgundy
>   Strive to be interress'd, what can you say to draw
>   A third more opulent than your sisters'? Speak.
>   *Cor.* Nothing, my lord.
>   *Lear.* Nothing?
>   *Cor.* Nothing.
>   *Lear.* Nothing will come of nothing, speak again.
>   *Cor.* Unhappy that I am, I cannot heave
>   My heart into my mouth. I love your Majesty
>   According to my bond, no more nor less.
>
>   (I.i.82–93)

What is Lear demanding, and why doesn't Cordelia give it to him? At this moment the great confusions of the play are set to explode. Cordelia, in the position of actually loving Lear, cannot summon the ability to *pretend* to love him. Instead, she is forced into a statement of her love as a public reckoning, a thoughtful, pondered calculation of what she owes the sovereign. This public reckoning humiliates Lear: its coldness, from one who loves him so warmly, reveals the sad hypocrisy of his demand. Yet Cordelia prefaces her statement with a report on her affective condition: "Unhappy that I am, I cannot heave / My heart into my mouth."

Cordelia cannot connect her heart to her words—she cannot put her love into words, and this is a result of her unhappiness. She is frozen, without words to say what she must not say. We might compare Cordelia's inability to move her heart to her mouth to Lear's inability to keep down his mother. Both of them suffer a disorder internal to the body that reaps tragic consequences. Why is Cordelia so unhappy? Is the humiliating demand placed upon her by Lear for a public performance in place of a private assurance an adequate explanation of her response to his demand for a public expression of love? Or is there a deeper pity that prevents her from imitating her older sisters? Is her relationship to her hypocritical sisters silencing her? Is her youth contributing to her stage fright? Of course, Cordelia is unhappy because she is humiliated, because she pities her father, because she is silenced, and because she is young.

But here again, a more thorough consideration of the missing mother may help explain the situation: it is the great absence in this drama. If Cordelia is motivated purely by love, is it enough to claim that Lear is motivated by his desire to avoid her pure love? We may imagine that *because* Cordelia cannot put her heart into her mouth, Lear cannot restrain the mother rising to his heart. His rage is motherly because Cordelia, by her very presence, cannot help reminding him that she is a motherless child and there is nothing he can do to repair that loss. While this tension frames the exchange between Lear and Cordelia, the problem of the missing mother enables the conflict between love and its avoidance to occur at the level of the motivation of these characters. The problem of the missing mother in the world of Shakespeare's play thus bears on the national tragedy that moves into our world in the post-Lear era.

Could it be that her acceptance is a refusal, and her refusal an acceptance? That she confounds us because she combines both? What is she refusing, and in her refusal, what is she affirming? What is she affirming, and in affirming, refusing? These questions admit no certain answers, but instead require a series of acknowledgments—of the force of love, the madness that love foments, the insistent demands we make for reassuring answers that our condition of true love seems to compel us to seek any time we are touched by it, and the lack of any adequate answer to our demands that also flows from our impossible attempts to truly love.

But there is even more to it than this, and it is the reason why the story of the fate of Cordelia prefaces this book on loneliness. We too live in the matrix of the missing mother, in the paradoxical context of no context, in the open world of storms into which we moderns have been cast. This is the way of loneliness. In her refusal to subject her love to the preordained claims of inheritance, the entailments that would lead her to live in the way of the court, Cordelia does not appeal to an unwritten law of kinship, as, for instance, her ancient predecessor Antigone may have; her act of refusal and her act of acceptance have as their most immediate consequence a disinheritance that throws her into the wilderness of politics. Nor is Cordelia's refusal an implicit claim to a deeper form of kinship, such as a restored matriarchy—if there ever was a matriarchy, it was abandoned with the death of her mother. What Cordelia seeks is a new way out of her family's drama of counterfeit love, a way into a sense of autonomy, which she tries to find through her attempt to establish a reasonable, rational, thoughtful division of love. She is refused that transition—a transition to a form of adulthood—by her abdicating father, but in spite of and because of that refusal she becomes the first lonely self. For Cordelia, loneliness becomes a way of life. She is thus our first modern person.

Cordelia overcomes her dumbness; she speaks with clarity and power, and the abyss opens for her and her father when she does. Her appeal is that of love, love that divides, as it must for the abdication to proceed honestly. When Cordelia insists that she will divide her love, she knows that this is how she will be true to her love of Lear. But he does not want her truth. How could he, being who he is, the sovereign, the united being who cannot divide his love as though it were real estate?

Imagine being Lear and listening to Cordelia's speech. Is there anything as heartbreaking for a father to hear as his daughter's measured response, her implicit suggestion that there is something unseemly about the way he has solicited love from her sisters, her all too mature claim that true love cannot, in the end, be "all," her insistence on returning love as a duty?

> *Cor.* Good my lord,
>   You have begot me, bred me, lov'd me; I
>   Return those duties back as are right fit,
>   Obey you, love you, and most honor you.
>   Why have my sisters husbands, if they say
>   They love you all? Happily, when I shall wed,
>   That lord whose hand must take my plight shall carry
>   Half my love with him, half my care and duty.
>   Sure I shall never marry like my sisters,
>   [To love my father all].
> *Lear.* But goes your heart with this?
> *Cor.* Ay, my good lord.
> *Lear.* So young, and so untender?

> *Cor.* So young, my lord, and true.
>
> *Lear.* Let it be so: thy truth then be thy dow'r!
>
> (I.i.95–108)

Lear's curse on Cordelia—"thy truth then be thy dow'r," a curse that silences all those present because of its sudden savagery—surely reflects the pain of a sovereign who cannot handle the truth of divided love. But there is something else he doesn't understand. Cordelia loves Lear beyond dutifulness, and her speech shows this because in dividing her love she is in a profound way imitating him—dividing her estate, which is composed of love, thus risking all by following him into the deep split that he has made within himself from the moment he decided to abdicate. Cavell says, "She is trying to conceal him; and to do that she cuts herself in two" (292). In doing so, she expresses the deepest and most ancient truth of modern life, that the divisions we are to enact between head and heart, heart and mouth, mother and heart, set us on a path that leads each one of us to isolation.

Half of Cordelia's love, being truthful, is worth infinitely more than the love of Regan and Goneril, which is no love at all. But Lear learns this too late, and Cordelia, full of this wisdom from the start, motherless child that she is, casts us as her descendants into an aberrant, unprecedented future. She speaks a new language, one of lonesomeness and longing, marking a path toward the healing of divisions of the self and the social that is, paradoxically, to define the isolated self of the modern era. Cordelia tells us this: Love is all we need to overcome absence—and loneliness is the absence we cannot overcome. This is the present in which we live.

It may be true that the divisions of love begun through the complex historical development of abdication and revolution were already apparent to Shakespeare's audience, that the great migration of sovereignty, the splitting of power from the absolute monarch into the souls of all of us, was well underway when Shakespeare first presented this tragedy at year's end in 1606, some four hundred years ago. But that moment is still alive to us now. It may also be that the calculus that Cordelia offered in the moment of her abandonment has indefinitely multiplied our occasions for tragedy as the selves of modern experience have divided and redivided, and as we fail to notice our ongoing tragedy in the pains of the everyday. (But it is not as though we now understand tragedy better for our experience of the everyday, if only because we still may not know enough of what the everyday is.) Writing about these occasions of pain and death, self-consciously referring us back to Lear's scene of abdication, Cavell returns us to our present presence. "We are present at these events," he writes, "and no one is present without making something happen; everything which is happening is happening to me, and I do not know what is happening. I do not know that my helplessness is limited only by my separateness, because I do not know which fortune is mine and which is yours. The world did not become sad; it was always sad. Tragedy has moved into the world, and with it the world becomes theatrical" (344).

Tragedy has moved into the world. This is the moment of the lonely self's ascendance. We are present at the place of our absence, lost in the stars, watching each other, waiting for each other to return from nowhere.

In this book I want to claim that being present at the place of our absence is what it means to experience loneliness. Is this loneliness merely nihilism? Much is made by many these days of the "nothings" of *King Lear*—how nothing comes of nothing; how Cordelia has nothing to say; how the Fool's breaking of the circle (the egg) to make two crowns foreshadows the dissolution of the Kingdom of nothing; how the abdication of Lear sets him on the road to nowhere; how any possible recovery is ruined through the death of all players of import, save Edgar, who matters so much primarily *be-*

cause only he survives, and secondarily because he "sullenly," that is, melancholically, survives, leading us to ask whether modern existence is to be essentially melancholic in character. These large questions led Harold Bloom to deify Shakespeare, hoping that this one great human would somehow be able to encompass our humanity, and hence to give the gnostic something to worship.

But the demands of philosophy are not those of faith. The thinkers I care about insist that there still may be something more to say about the truth we live, and insist upon the fact that we are to *live* that something. Truth is our dowry, just as it is Cordelia's.[4] But the truth we have inherited has led us to another place. This book was written across a period of time when the United States fought one war to avenge terrorist killings on American soil, and embarked on another war in a quest for a new empire, leaving us again in a quagmire, showing even ourselves how this country has become the most dangerous nation in the world. In this time our lying leaders generate new falsehoods everyday. So it turns out that we need to rely upon Cordelia's dowry to help us resist the prospect of an ever-widening experience of twenty-first-century war.

There are enormous questions that we ask in and of the world that have been unanswered in the void that opened at the tip of the island of Manhattan on September 11, 2001, a void that by the time of this writing has come to replicate itself on a larger scale in the heart of Baghdad and that sometimes seems to threaten to swallow the entire world. How are we to grieve? What should we be demanding of ourselves? What have we to do with the terror that afflicts the world? Rather than confront this void, our sovereign authorities have lashed out, as mad as Lear in all his fury, and now we suffer from the spread of a new shame. What we have come to expect of the world is now denied to us by the actions of those whom we have permitted to be placed in charge of our lives. How we respond to those acts of denial may in the end determine questions of war and peace, in fact may determine such matters more than the strategies of generals and fanatics, who are always already ready for war, always ready to kill, to torture, to imprison, to silence, regardless of their very real reluctance to do so. This is still the claim that thinkers make on the world, to speak the truth of our ongoing shame in the face of a tragedy born of a powerful powerlessness, a tragedy born of a new avoidance of love.

The lonely self is born within this matrix, in the face of it—suppressed by it, and yet responsive to it. There is always a turn to be made, no matter how unlimited the question, no matter how powerful the hurt, how deep the harm. Here we are, still unable to abdicate. Still unable to love. What are we waiting for? Tragedy has moved into the world as the certainties of sovereignty have crumbled. Cordelia's truthfulness enabled this passage to modernity. Like her, we need to confront this enormous fact without embarrassment and without shrinking from its philosophical import, not only for the sake of the future, but for the sake of rethinking who we are and how we may be present in our present.

Recognizing the fatality of the division of Cordelia's love, can we learn other affective ways of attaching ourselves to the world? This is, in fact, to be our task, ongoing. Through the family discord of Cordelia and Lear, Shakespeare provided us denizens of the twenty-first century with an ancient key for beginning to see who we are. Cordelia can divide her love, but she cannot divide herself. Lear can have absolute power or the love of his child, but he cannot have both. And in their attempts to overcome the divisions of the self that they improvise in order to escape unbearable circumstances, they reflect our lesser struggles to become who we are in the face of our more quotidian, but every bit as painful circumstances. They reflect the fundamental fact of loss, of a wife, of a mother, of a very real and profound love that has gone missing from their world, and from ours.

We too are lonely selves. We too have much to learn, and we risk the tragic fate of those who fail to learn in time. And yet we still have all the time in the world—a world, it seems, that is always coming to an end. The claims we make upon our tragic world are also inevitably personal in character. For all of us there are grievances we cannot resolve, recognitions we try our best to avoid, coincidences of folly that leave us either laughing or in a puddle of tears, all of these reflected in the things we think and write about. As will become clear, I do not offer myself as an exception to this rule, but rather as a proof. Like many others, I may go to my grave crying over my missing mother.

And if I am lucky, my motherless children will be there when I die. For you see, my thoughts about the missing mother are not the result of cool observation, but a fact of my life. My own mother was, as a result of circumstances I will explore in this book, unable to be present for me as I wanted her to be. More immediately, my daughter Irene and her younger brother Jimmy lost their own mother to death several years ago, while I was beginning to work on this book. So my convictions about the relationship of Lear and Cordelia are informed by my own losses and my ongoing attempt to mother my motherless children, to address the sorrow of this ordinary loss in the context of a present formed by the larger experience of a political culture shaped by loss. The intensity of this experience has afforded me a perspective that has driven me onward as I have tried to follow it to its root, a spiral of thought and feeling that I will be retracing throughout the following pages.

I tell you these details from my life because I suspect that if you have picked up this book, you are asking pertinent questions about what it means to be lonely, and in turn I believe that it is my charge to explain myself to you as fully as I can in order for you to understand how and why I came to think about this subject as I do. In the chapters that follow I will be thinking, in light of Cordelia's calculus, about how we are in the world (Being), how we attempt to hold the world (Having), how we desire (Loving), and how we suffer loss (Grieving). In all of these ever-shifting groundings of the experience of loneliness we may find ourselves retreating to some inner ocean, seeking repair through reliance on a self not yet attained. This is a quest and a question for us. What are we to become as we live our lives, how are we to live with ourselves and each other? How are we to live with loneliness as our way of life?

Chapter I

Being

Oh lonely death on lonely life.
—Captain Ahab, in Melville, *Moby-Dick*

The All One

It isn't as if Shakespeare invented loneliness, as brilliantly as he narrated its emerging force in the modern era. Think again of Cordelia and her dad, and imagine some words that might describe their common plight. *Exiled, untouched, ignored, isolated, desolated, alienated, outcast, denied, lost, mad.* Is it too much to claim that this list of words summarizes something important about all of us? Each one of us confronts an interminable ocean, a place untouchable by others, a language that sounds to us like a scream in the night. We imagine that to be alone is the worst we can experience. But how has it come to pass that we think this way? Why do we find such pain in the experience of being alone? Where does this pain come from? And why are we so attached to it? What pleasure is in it for us? Is the pleasure of being alone only painful?

We theorists sometimes seek meaning in the etymologies of words. In this circumstance, it is powerfully apparent how the evolution of our language bears upon the subject of loneliness. The word "alone" is formed of the compound of two words, "all" and "one." The All—the absolute containment of the inside on the outside; the One—the absolute containment of the outside on the inside. Floating through undifferentiated space, and yet pregnant with a sense of self, we fly into a universe both unmarked and yet totally defined. We are motivated; we are lost in space. "I am all one," we say, triumphant and desperate. The All One condemns us to being no more than a weed in the wall at the same time as it allows us to be the most powerful of sovereigns. For being alone is not only the worst we can experience; it is also the inevitable moment of some of our greatest experiences. In the solitude of our selves we learn something that is otherwise unavailable to us—how to become who we are. This is no small accomplishment. This other experience of being alone is what Ralph Waldo Emerson once called self-trust, and it leads to a way of life that is worth our while, despite the pain we may experience, the heartache of thinking that we will never know another as we know ourselves.

Being alone. I confess that I think more often of the worst of the experience of being alone than I do of the best; I focus on the trauma and pain of the experience of deep isolation, a state of a certain kind of despair, rather than the greater pleasures of solitude and self-reliance. And yet as hard as I struggle to imagine the one without the other, the pain without the pleasure, I realize that the two emotional states are inextricably connected. So why do I think about the pain first? It is undoubtedly an idiosyncrasy, but I believe it is fortunate that I feel this way, because putting the pain first also has a practical use. It is from the margins that we can see the center more clearly; it is from the perspective of what Michel Foucault once characterized as the "perverse implantation" that we may better observe what we call normal. In the state of crisis induced by the pain of being alone, it is more likely that we will clearly see the motives and ends of the lonely self, even when that self moves from despair to happier ways of being.

The inclination of modern life, with its distractions and shallowness, obscures the deeper fact of our separation from each other. So we need to establish a certain distance from our distractions in order to think more clearly about what it is we are seeking from each other. It is in the silence that we may come to recognize the fact of our ghostly existence, our fatal separation from each other, and from our better selves. And yet it is this separation that we must preserve so as to come to understand the dangers that accompany our ongoing attempts to overcome it.

How, then, may we consider this state of being alone? From the start we may know that loss awaits us all—diminishment, states of gracelessness, harm, wound, detachment. But in order to hew close to the truths that loneliness has to tell, to try to excavate its meaning for being human, we need to move beyond the terms that shape our discussions of it as currently configured. I want to test the terms and conditions of the experience of loneliness in another way, so that we may try to reckon whether or not it is worthy of our lives to continue to live on in the way of the All One. This is a test that Henry David Thoreau, among others, has taught us to take—to ask whether we should resign ourselves to living in a particular way, especially when it becomes clear to us that such a way of life means that we risk looking back upon our lives only to realize that we haven't really lived.

The question of loneliness entails imagining how it is that we are facing or confronting the world. Thus I explore the loneliness of the person I am supposed to know best, me. It is true that I'm more interested in *how* I am these days than in *who* I am, and even as I retain some interest in who I am, I'm more interested in who I am becoming than in who I have been. But I intend these developments in my experiential life to be coincident with yours. That is to say, my self-interest extends to you, because I take seriously Whitman's striving to be a part of something that could be called a greater thing; because I understand that self-reliance is itself a process of becoming that depends upon conversation with companions, helpmeets, friends; because it is a paradoxical truth that there is no escaping our selves, and that a proper care of the self is likely to be the best way of joining with others. My particular song of self is inflected through a lens of decline, a forceful sense that the ordinary experience of life has become increasingly endangered as forces of normalization and spectacle suck our internal resources dry, leaving us alone in a way that is increasingly difficult to overcome. The question of decline—of our culture, of our selves, of our knowledge of our lives in common and apart—is, I believe, how the problem of loneliness presents itself to us in our time. (We are still, in this sense, the heirs of Cordelia, in that the matrix of loneliness remains the matrix of the missing mother.)

Despite the enormous literature, despite the constant discussion of the condition of loneliness, I don't think most of us have yet appreciated the complexity of lonely being as a distinctly modern phenomenon. Our way of thinking about liberal freedom, its shallowness, its threadbare quality, and yet its persistence and power over centuries, has taught me how little I know about loneliness in this regard. But I am aware of the fact that the lonely self has been at the heart of an immense cultural, political, and philosophical edifice, an aspect of all that we experience as humans, of how we come to know ourselves and the world we inhabit. So I want to try to do what others have attempted to do, which is, simply put, to think about what it means to be alone.

There has been a drumbeat of news—for the past fifty years at least, if you want to call that news—concerning how lonely we Americans are in our increasingly complex society. This literature has been a constant feature of sociology and the political study of civil society. Simply to list some of the most prominent of these books is to describe a syllabus containing some of the most important works in the history of American sociology.[1] These studies are united by a common premise: that there is a deficiency or lack of connection to others that has become the defining characteristic of a particular class, gender, race and/or even generational cohort who are perceived to be the exemplars of the relevant ordinary person under examination. For most of these scholars, this ordinary person is defined by a timid introspection that turns away from common concern to the pursuit of a selfish life. From several ideological perspectives, all of these authors have documented one or another variety of retreat into private life and have construed this retreat as a threat to something they identify as the common good. Sometimes embracing nostrums uncomfortably close to the most culturally reactionary formulas available, or explicitly urging a revival of religious brotherhood, or incoherently insisting upon a greater "investment" in "social capital," they proffer solutions that are, at their best, mildly liberating and helpful in their own ways, but nevertheless are not commensurate with the scope and depth of the problem posed by loneliness at its deepest level. Alas, it may be that this incommensurability is the most telling element of these studies. (While it is certainly not the case that only American scholars have been concerned with the problem of loneliness, as should become clear when I explore the contribution of Hannah Arendt to this subject, there is a way in which the split between European and Anglo-American philosophy has its parallel in the ways in which the concern with loneliness is expressed. For many European thinkers the self is already to be scrutinized as subject to the conditions of its cultivation. For Americans, a stubborn core of agency and volition gives shape to the ways in which the problem of loneliness is approached, less as a social problem and more as one of personal circumstance.)

Rather than engaging the work of these scholars, I want to take another direction. I am concerned with what we might call domains of life—structural situations in which the feeling of loneliness comes to the fore, and out of which people react or respond to their lonely condition. One might say I am interested in the condition of the souls of lonely people, in the sense that my concern is not to predict behavior but to understand better the existential situations of people as they struggle to come to terms with who they are and how they are in a world in which they feel they are more or less alone. If, as Foucault once claimed, the soul is the prison of the body, then I may be thought of as exploring that soul, that prison, in an attempt to reflect on how we might, if not escape its most powerful strictures, then at least begin to renegotiate the terms of our confinement.[2]

Thinking about Being Lonely

So what does it mean to be lonely? This is a simple question, but it admits no simple answer. While loneliness is close to being a universal experience of human life, for many reasons it is not easy to describe. However, certain generally accepted truths concerning the human condition might serve as guideposts for discussion. For instance, we may note that to be human is to risk being alone in a way that is unbidden and unwanted. And we may also note that while we are alive, we humans search for what we imagine our world to be. It is true that from the start of our lives and for our lives' duration, we seek others to comfort us, harm us, ignore us, and move us onto our paths through and out of life. Loneliness is deeply entangled in all paths of life because it reveals in sharp profile some of the most important limits of who we are and how we are with each other. It may be said that loneliness is fundamental to the very constitution of our selves.

There are moments when we find it astonishing, this life. We are astonished at least in part because we know of no other life and yet we retain a capacity to be amazed by the singularity of this one. It seems as though each of us is endowed with the ability to think of our life specifically as being *this* life, and we are able to do so without any direct experience of other lives with which we may make a comparison. The endowment of this life is a core paradox of our existence that motivates great religious thoughts, generates extraordinary imaginative energies, and underwrites profound philosophical discourses. Yet for much of the living of it, we try to avoid thinking about this life. We move about the world obscurely ashamed of our pretense, embarrassed by our unbidden participation in the search for meaning beyond the conventions handed down to us. We intuit that to face this life at the most basic level would be to experience a sort of sublime terror. Many of us would do almost anything, even deny our own life, to avoid that feeling. We cling to the familiar, even as a part of each of us remains acquainted with a strangeness inside ourselves. The world of our familiar takes on many modes that are deeply rooted in the rhythms of the everyday, and we say to ourselves that this is the world we live in. Yet this world remains largely unthought. It is as if we are condemned to see life retrospectively. In such moments, life itself seems like a broken clock that can be taken apart and truly known only when it no longer keeps time.

This is one way we come to know ourselves. But this way of knowing kills its object and violates what would seem to be our paramount responsibility of caring for ourselves. The care of the self is always related to *how* we know ourselves, how we explore and whether we decide to investigate the grounding of our life. And yet this care has another end in mind than knowing; it entails an acknowledgment of the very limits of what we may know while appreciating that there may still be an unknown that must remain unknown. How deeply we go in pursuit of this form of caring is not settled by rules, nor by the commands of various orthodoxies. Moreover, we cannot absolve ourselves of this obscure responsibility of caring for ourselves by consigning this work to philosophers. As a matter of basic human right and responsibility, philosophizing is not an activity that is limited to those who are designated as philosophers. The thinking person, as Emerson suggests in his essay on

the American scholar, is anyone who faintly remembers the whole-
ness of a world that we can only experience partially. While we can
never overcome this partiality, we still seek ways to endure it and to
find something certain or energizing about our selves from within
its bounds. We try different therapies that would comfort us in the
face of our shattered condition or that would help us cope with or
evade the harm we otherwise would suffer.

Loneliness is one of the ways we experience partiality. We can
never experience the world as a whole because we are mortal. We
are fated to seek assurances for our existence, even though such assurances can never overcome our basic doubt. We negotiate a path
through this life with others, both with those who are far outside of
us and with those who have penetrated our interiors. We hear voices
composed of the fragments of those others, we speak, we listen, we
touch and are touched, and we always fail to achieve an understanding that would allow us to rest. Our unending desires remain unsat-
isfied. Yet our failures, as inevitable as they are, also shape whatever
our successes may be. We move through life, and our lives are
shaped by these movements.

When the reach of our selves to others becomes so fragmented
and confused that we find ourselves arrested, or halted, or otherwise blocked from contact with them and from ourselves, we become lonely. We may thus think of loneliness as the experience of
unhappy removal from a life lived in common with others.

How we are removed from the presence of others would constitute a politics of loneliness. But because loneliness involves our removal from others, it has sometimes been construed by political
thinkers as having nothing to do with the political condition of a
society. Rather, it is read as a sign of the evacuation of meaning or
politics from life. Aristotle once characterized a person who is un-
connected to the polity as *idiotes,* a term which survives in vernacu-
lar English as the word "idiot," and which in its plainest context

means someone who is isolated from all others, unable to speak the common language, unable to interact. It was questionable for Aristotle whether such a person—someone cut off from participation in the *polis*—could even be considered a human being. But to understand loneliness as unpolitical is a mistake, even in the guise of describing it as a casting out of polity. Loneliness can never be reduced to being merely a necessary contrast to the condition of political existence. What seemed to Aristotle a dividing line between polity and idiocy has never been an absolute frontier, and the line has been breached many times. It may even be the case that the terms of modern political identities are shaped by the inevitable crossings of public and private, that this line has become a blur.

In a political sense, loneliness may be thought of as a sign, perhaps the most important sign, of the ghostly presence of an almost effaced distinction between the public and private realms of life. The very texture of modern life is inflected by loneliness. It is a leading experience through which we shape our perceptions of the world. It informs our deepest longings and aversions, an element infiltrating every part of our existence. Loneliness thus may be thought of as being a profoundly political experience because it is instrumental in the shaping and exercise of power, the meaning of individuality, and the ways in which justice is to be comprehended and realized in the world.

Of course we could employ other terms as well. For instance, we could say that contemporary civilization is built upon the foundation of a deep estrangement that we experience more or less in common, and that the sources of this common estrangement may be found in the shaping by our own hands of certain institutions concerned with the governance of polity, economy, social life, and self. We could use the sociological terms "alienation" or "anomie." But all these categories of distinction may be traced back to a common root: all are expressions of a deeper loneliness which they inadequately capture. Loneliness may be thought of as foundational, in the sense that in the end we all understand ourselves as being alone in the world. While being alone is not itself synonymous with loneliness, and while estrangement or alienation takes on forms other than loneliness, it is equally true that the rise of modern loneliness more than coincides with harmful experiences of being alone.

Although the progress or regress of representative democracy, a paramount political institution of modern life, is closely related to the experience of loneliness, it may be that, as in the relationship of loneliness to estrangement, the relationship between loneliness and democracy cannot be plotted in any direct sense. For instance, I understand myself to be a democrat and a liberal, as these terms are commonly understood today. I am committed to substantive and procedural equality and to the protection of the rights of individuals to life, liberty, and the pursuit of happiness. Less conventionally, I am also committed to certain elements of democracy and liberalism that are not commonly understood to be essential to their definition and realization in the world. In this regard my liberal commitment to individual rights is a consequence of what I reckon to be the historically contingent inevitability of individual embodiment: to the extent that the right to pursue happiness must still be acknowledged as an individual right, then the political doctrine of liberalism is inevitably a sentimental one in its most primitive meaning, that of having to do with the senses. Because of the corporeality of life, a robust liberalism must be connected to the way we encourage or discourage certain ways of thinking, feeling, and acting about our affective connections and disconnections to our selves and others. Foucault understood the various ways we attend to embodiment to be important forms of the care of the self.

I understand democracy as not only a good in and of itself, nor

even primarily as the vehicle for the realization of a distributive justice of substantive goods, but as a means toward the end of developing a more robust sense of the connections between self and others that may enable a happier and less lonesome way of being in the
world. This vision of democracy is what William E. Connolly has
sought to attain in thinking through what he calls the ethos of pluralization. That is, democracy may be thought of as a way of shaping discourse and deliberation so as to allow us to reflect and act
upon highly variegated ideas of the common good associated with
affective freedom, so that the arts of being free may be commonly
encouraged and their sphere of influence enlarged. It is, in Thoreau's sense, a tradition.

When democracy and liberalism enable each other in this way,
the result is a marvelously rich matrix, a culture for living our life in
common and in solitude. But of course we must ask, when has it
ever been thus? There is a great paradox here in the experience of
liberal democracy, because loneliness is both a fulfillment and a dis-
ruption of its possibility. This paradox gives shape to what we may
think of as a dangerous politics of the self, a politics potentially de-
structive of freedom and the possibilities of equality. To consider
how loneliness has become a predominant affective connection of
self to other in the modern era is to ask what the fact of lonely being has meant for us. Loneliness is a condition that rebukes the
ambitions of the pious and profane alike: whatever ameliorating
schemes have been offered by today's public intellectuals to heal the
harms that have resulted from economic, racial, and gender in-
equality, social isolation, violence, war, and weakened civil society,
they are shadowed by the fundamental condition of lonely being.[3]

But if the problem of loneliness lies deeper than the solutions
proffered by these American thinkers, the difficulty may be attri-
buted not so much to any specific deficiency in their analyses as to
an elusive element in the quality of the problem itself. Loneliness is

both so common an experience and so tied to psychic life as to make the attempt to describe it paradoxical as well, for loneliness itself involves a failure of the self-descriptive capacity. Like the experience of physical pain, it may somehow be beyond words. Indeed, loneliness may be a kind of pain. Elaine Scarry implicitly makes the comparison when she writes of the isolating, world-destroying power of pain.[4] Pain grows and the world shrinks. Loneliness isolates in a different way: rather than destroying the world, it establishes a barrier between the self and the world, leaving the world intact as a torment to the isolated person. Loneliness grows and the world recedes, eventually disappearing over the horizon. Will the world ever appear again? Was it ever there in the first place? (This is a kind of madness, what may be thought of as a madness bequeathed to us by Descartes.) And again, like pain, loneliness must be thought of as a necessary part of experience.

Despite the muteness into which our loneliness leads us, words are still a potent way, perhaps the most effective way, to gain access to the experience of loneliness. The fact that we have words as instruments to describe what may be indescribable is paradoxical. But we do things with words all the time, without always knowing what it is we are doing. That this lack of self-knowledge, if that is indeed what it is, so often is seen as a failure may be no more than a result of our blind pessimism—our suspicion that there is a failure of meaning itself—*and* our equally blind optimism—the failure to achieve certain meaning enables us to fantasize a perfection always only slightly out of reach. We ought to eschew both moods, to the extent that we can, when trying to think through our condition. Moreover, there is another way in which we may think of our words.[5] As constituted in sentences and paragraphs and other fragments (for, as Thoreau suggests and Deleuze emphasizes, there is no such thing as a *single* word), our words shape and are shaped by forces that materialize our spiritual lives.

For example, let us reconsider a sentence from a few pages back:

When democracy and liberalism enable each other in this way, the result is a marvelously rich matrix, a culture for living our life in common and in solitude.

Does it make a difference to you to realize that the word *matrix* was once the word used to describe the womb, and became, through the magic of metonymy, a synonym for the word *mother?* Attentive to this word because of Lear and his struggle to contain his rising mother, I came to this etymological discovery in the notes to the *Riverside Shakespeare*. But why did it catch my attention? The fact that I am concerned about the problem of the missing mother in Lear, but also elsewhere, for reasons that extend to my personal concerns about marriage and death, motherless children, and the changing moods of the widower that I am, also may or may not be of relevance to your understanding of the word. And yet I think it would be very strange, once this knowledge of the word and my uses of it is gained, to believe that your further encounters with the word would not somehow be influenced by your new understanding. For me it would also be strange to think about the word *matrix* in a sentence without associating democracy and liberalism with an entire set of arguments concerning the relationship of marriage and remarriage to relationships of consent, or with Thoreau's accounting of consent through rituals of resigning and refusal, resistance and acquiescence.[6] Moreover, to imagine that democracy and liberalism may be wedded to each other, nurturing a space for natality and renewal, a feminizing movement, a cultural expression of embodied love, could help move us beyond the mechanical calculus of happiness and duty in our considerations of how we are to rule ourselves.

If such a resonance is possible concerning the positioning of one word embedded in one sentence, what about the more complex experience of lonely being? It would seem that we are faced with an extraordinarily difficult task of description that entails, not control over meaning or a probing for final truths, but a continuing acknowledgment that the truths of our lives will never be governed completely by the imperatives of rules, and—what is perhaps more surprising—that democracy itself depends upon the continuing and autonomous iteration and reiteration of the meaning of words, sentences, paragraphs, and fragments. Instead of reaching final conclusions, perhaps we would do better to think in terms of the rituals of truth that govern our lives together and apart, truths that are radically historical in character.

However we choose to think about the experience of loneliness, no specific emphasis on one aspect of it can be thought of as final. The difficulty is that loneliness is presented to us as a termination point, as a finality, as an ending. So it remains for me to do what I acknowledge may not be possible—to describe what cannot be described, to define that which exceeds definition, to write in such a way as to encourage further movement away from endings and toward beginnings. This is a seemingly immodest ambition, but it is also the most ordinary task we humans undertake in our lives together.

The Pathos of Disappearance

To begin, a provisional definition:

Loneliness is the experience of the pathos of disappearance.

We are marked by loneliness when we register the death of others to us, when we cease to be connected to the things that surround us, and when we notice that we somehow have become something that we no longer recognize as ourselves. Loneliness is akin to the experience of skepticism. Its intellectual affect suggests a gesture toward doubting the very possibility that the world we inhabit actually exists. In this radical doubt, loneliness may well be considered as a side effect of Cartesian doubt, the spread of a terrible thought Descartes had in his study when he came to question his own existence. But we know that loneliness is a condition that is shared more or less by all who have ever lived as humans (and perhaps by other animals as well—I believe my dog is sometimes lonely when I am gone and he is alone), even as it is distinguished in a new way in the modern era, in that one of the most prominent experiences that we share is our very separation and estrangement from each other and the world.

That loneliness is an experience of pathos reveals it, paradoxically, to be rooted in the most explicit social and cultural structures of ordinary life. The pathos of loneliness is its path through language and the limits of language—that is, it is a well-marked or reiterated narrative that assumes an aura of (tragic) inevitability in human life. Because loneliness is an experience of disappearance, it is embedded in existential paradoxes concerning the meaning of life as a death-bound experience. We appear on life's stage, and then we disappear. The realm of appearances—of representations of life— that is inspired by the condition of loneliness suggests that we will find eloquent expression of the condition of loneliness in the common vernaculars of life. In short, the boundaries commonly said to separate the psychological, social, and ontological dimensions of life are blurred by the experience of loneliness.

Within the bounds of the condition of loneliness we are able to bear existence, or even more, we are happily able to inhabit our world through the multiple constructions of our extraordinarily rich inner lives, which keep us going when other persons fail us, as, being mortal, they inevitably must. Others fail us because nobody is perfect. Interestingly, in the modern era we have attached this idea of imperfection to the fact of embodiment, for we now see death itself as a form of failure, as a mistake of some sort. If it has always been the case that each and every one of us must die, it has not always been the case that failure has so ubiquitously attached itself to the experience of death. This spreading sense of failure, along with our techniques for overcoming or bearing or subverting it, constitutes a large part of who we are now. Loneliness is a lens through which we may read the world around us as a failure.

Total Abandonment

Some aspects of this sketch of loneliness may be familiar to those who have read the work of Hannah Arendt concerning totalitarianism and modern life.[7] In the concluding pages of *The Origins of Totalitarianism,* Arendt argues that totalitarianism is to be distinguished from other forms of tyranny in large part by the way it cultivates, through rule by terror, a widespread, almost universal loneliness among the citizens of a state. This is not to say she was arguing that the form of rule determined whether there would be loneliness, but only that totalitarianism enforces and encourages loneliness as a means of securing and perpetuating its mode of rule.

Arendt discussed loneliness in the context of her comments concerning the relationship of terror and ideology. For her, terror, "the essence of totalitarian domination . . . is the realization of the law of movement; its chief aim is to make it possible for the force of nature or of history to race freely through mankind, unhindered by any spontaneous human action" (OT, 464–465). For the movement of total rule to make progress, mere humans must be held in check, which is what total terror does: "[Total terror] substitutes for the boundaries and channels of communication between individual men a band of iron which holds them so tightly together that it is as though their plurality had disappeared into One Man of gigantic dimensions" (OT, 465–466). This One Man is the All One writ large, a Leviathan of loneliness. Totalitarian government relies

upon the extraordinary condition of stillness—a lack of free movement—to control those who live under its rule. "It destroys the one
essential prerequisite of all freedom which is simply the capacity of
motion which cannot exist without space" (OT, 466). To put it another way, totalitarian rule is marked by the ability of its adminis-
trators to destroy the space between individuals through which
people act as free subjects.

The problem with such a conceptualization of space, however, is
that in everyday human terms space is not neutral and unmarked,
an open and infinite entity; it is shaped by people as they interact
through, under, and outside of demarcated social fields of life.
Much like the great liberal philosopher Isaiah Berlin, who had a
similar blind spot in thinking about space, Arendt both recognized
this complexity and adhered to a strangely unmarked understanding of space. She understood how totalitarian ideologies provide
complete explanations for reality detached from experience, how
they are backed by the force of rule through terror, and hence are
capable of actually changing reality for those who are subjected to
them through an iron logic impervious to the messiness of ordinary
life. For her, this combination of ideology and terror is the signature of totalitarian rule.

But by failing to recognize the complexities of space, Arendt limits her vision. The totalitarian imagination that she saw as all-en-
compassing was not simply to be confronted with a reassertion of a
public sphere where action could take place. Indeed, the more nu-
anced and differentiated development of alternative spaces that
provided sustenance and aid to those who would exercise freedom
even within the terrible confines of such rule was to be the constitutive power that eventually eroded totalitarian systems. The iron
band always has its weak points—cracks and fissures which contribute to its breakdown. It is the exploration of those often hidden
spaces that enables democratic negotiations, the possibility of what
we may call a politics of becoming. The public that Arendt admires

so much is cultivated by ordinary people as they work through the complex processes of economy and society. But in her elevation of action as the quintessence of politics, she implicitly denigrated those realms of human existence.

Yet in focusing on the worst, Arendt provides us with an illumination of the political effect of loneliness. At its worst, loneliness is a denial of the possibility of a politics of becoming. Arendt rightly believed that at the heart of totalitarianism is the experience of a deep loneliness. While she was concerned about the isolation of people resulting from the devices of totalitarian rule, she also noted that it is possible to be isolated from others without being lonely. She argued that the key power of totalitarianism is its capacity to invade the sphere of the social, destroying any semblance of a public/private distinction, and, from her perspective, destroying the possibility of political action as well. Loneliness was thus for her the destruction of social space through the erasure of the public/private distinction.

Arendt also noted that the experience of isolation—of being unable to connect with others in public to act in concert—is an ordinary experience of life. She presented the example of *homo faber,* the creative worker who leaves, if only temporarily, the realm of politics in order to focus on his task of building a world of things. Using categories of experience that she was later to develop in *The Human Condition,* she wrote, "Tyranny based on isolation generally leaves the productive capacities of man intact; a tyranny over 'laborers,' however, as for instance the rule over slaves in antiquity, would automatically be a rule over lonely, not only isolated, men and tend to be totalitarian" (OT, 475). In this sense, loneliness is a more encompassing affective state than is simple isolation, or, as Arendt puts it, "Loneliness concerns human life as a whole" (OT, 475). Moreover, loneliness reaches a particularly dangerous tipping point in the annals of experience when our world is dominated by labor, by the retreat (or advance) to an emphasis on the reproductive capacity of a human being. Hence any totalitarian government, in contrast to a mere tyranny, will reach beyond the power to isolate and will drive its subjects into a state of pervasive loneliness.

As labor came to be fragmented and dissipated in late modernity, forces of identity came to the fore. While Arendt did not fully recognize this development—her comment concerning Little Rock and the civil rights movement was only the most notorious instance of her blindness in that regard—she did anticipate the quest for identity in a negative way. She suggested that loneliness derives from a condition of being superfluous that grows out of uprootedness, the lacking of a place in the world that is "recognized and guaranteed by others" (OT, 475). She argued,

> Taken by itself, without consideration of its recent historical causes and its new role in politics, loneliness is at the same time contrary to the basic requirements of the human condition *and* one of the fundamental experiences of every human life. Even the experience of the materially and sensually given world depends upon my being in contact with other men, upon our *common* sense which regulates and controls all other senses and without which each of us would be enclosed in his own particularity of sense data which in themselves are unreliable and treacherous. Only because we have common sense, that is only because not one man, but men in the plural inhabit the earth can we trust our immediate sensual experience. Yet we have only to remind ourselves that one day we shall have to leave this common world which will go on as before and for whose continuity we are superfluous in order to realize loneliness, the experience of being abandoned by everything and everybody. (OT, 475–476)

Rather than imagine the development of new forms of identity politics through which new mediations of the common might be developed, Arendt followed a more austere path. Her observation that loneliness is a condition in which we cannot trust our sensual experience echoes the claim that René Descartes made in his *Meditations* when he elaborated the meaning of the *cogito*. For her, Cartesianism, as a departure from common sense, contributes to the corrosive power of a skepticism that throws us into doubt about the very existence of others outside of ourselves, those we must depend upon to aid us in trusting our "sensual experience."

It is as though the moment of philosophical insight that resulted in the idea of the *cogito* has spread as a historical infection, overwhelming the world as we attempt to live in common after the death of God—in fact contributing to God's death by elevating skepticism to its permanent position over faith. The working through of this skepticism in everyday experience, what Stanley Cavell calls "living our skepticism," turns us toward understanding loneliness as a way of life, a life in which we are unable to recognize ourselves with the sort of certainty that would allow us to join with others, rather than conform to them. It is in conformity that we become ghostly, uncertain of ourselves because we are unable to think about how we are alone, even as we realize that we are alone. We lose ourselves in ourselves.

This is what could be called the pathology of loneliness. In Arendt's definition of loneliness—the experience of being abandoned by everything and everybody—a particular pathos is associated with the secular anticipation of a singular event, our own death. Loneliness is not death. Yet we might as well be dead when our only possibility is to be alone, because the worst aspect of loneliness is that it ends the possibility of meaningful experience by translating the inner dialogue of solitude into a monologue of desolation. As the quintessential condition of singularity, loneliness is unlike the condition of solitude, although, unless the world becomes so bleak as to be irremediable to us, we hold out the hope that we may emerge from loneliness into solitude. In solitude, we are each of us by our self, but not yet alone, because we are more or less happily occupied with our self, beside our self in a positive way, or in Arendt's term, two-in-one. To move from loneliness to solitude is to recover the world we have lost.

The two-in-one is in strong contrast to the All One, the state of being alone. When we are lonely we are actually alone, deserted by all others, including our own other self (OT, 476).

> What makes loneliness so unbearable is the loss of one's own self which can be realized in solitude, but confirmed in its identity only by the trusting and trustworthy company of my equals. In this situation, man loses trust in himself as the partner of his thoughts, and that elementary confidence in the world which is necessary to make experiences at all. Self and world, capacity for thought and experience are lost at the same time. (OT, 477)

The state of loneliness as one-ness, Arendt claimed, was once common but very temporarily felt. Though she called loneliness an experience, it is an experience composed of a loss of the capacity to experience. It is important to note that if we accept her definition of experience, we cannot say that we are even having an experience at the moment we are lonely (OT, 477). This problem is what one might call the paradox of experience, its uselessness, its disconnection from the world.

Perhaps even more significantly, Arendt argued that loneliness emerges as a permanent condition first for those who are philosophers; she cited Hegel's deathbed pronouncement, "Nobody has understood me except one; and he also misunderstood" (OT, 477). By the twentieth century, however, loneliness has escaped the confines of philosophical experience and has become the everyday experience of "the ever growing masses" (OT, 478). Exploiting the massification of modern Western societies, totalitarianism is so terrible because it uses loneliness as an instrument of rule and blocks any paths leading back from loneliness into solitude. It embraces us in an isolation that desolates—an isolation that goes the whole way down.

"We Refugees"

For Arendt, loneliness was not only a useful term for capturing the essence of an instrument of totalitarian rule; it was also a profound element of her experience as an assimilated European Jew who had to accommodate herself to the continual status of refugee. In an essay from 1943, entitled "We Refugees," Arendt goes beyond describing the function of loneliness and dwells within it.[8] This is an unusual essay for her, because here she speaks directly to questions concerning the shaping of her own identity, the wounds she has suffered, the deep harm that comes from having her value as a human being called into question, not only by the likes of Hitler and his government of thugs, but by a world that, through complacency and complicity, condemns the refugee to the status of refugee. But even as Arendt directly addresses the terms of her own experience, she still speaks in the first person plural, understanding "we refugees" to be a synonym for the pariah Jew that she is.

Arendt begins with reflections on the optimism of her fellow refugees, the idea of optimism in the face of loss. What losses have these refugees suffered? She patiently lists them. The loss of home, which means the familiarity of daily life. The loss of occupation, which means a sense of usefulness in the world. The loss of first language, which means naturalness of expression, simplicity of gesture, and unaffected expression of feelings. And finally, the loss of relatives and friends, those killed in concentration camps, the rupture of private lives. In the face of these losses, optimism is an attempt at forgetting, an embrace of the new and repudiation of the past. "The more optimistic among us would even add that their whole former life had been passed in a kind of unconscious exile and only their new country now taught them what home really looks like." This forgetting was important, because it was necessary for everyone to suppress the knowledge that contemporary history created "a new kind of human being—the kind that are put into concentration camps by their foes and in internment camps by their friends" (265).

As the essay unfolds, this optimism becomes a token of despair. Thinking about the night thoughts of her fellow refugees, who may be wondering whether their new countrymen may turn on them as their former ones did, Arendt writes, "I dare not ask for information, since I, too, had rather be an optimist" (266). But for some, it is not possible to forget some things.

> There are those odd optimists among us who, having made a lot of optimistic speeches, go home and turn on the gas or make use of a skyscraper in quite an unexpected way. They seem to prove that our proclaimed cheerfulness is based on a dangerous readiness for death. Brought up in the conviction that life is the highest good and death the greatest dismay, we became witnesses and victims of worse terrors than death—without having been able to discover a higher ideal than life. (266)

This turn, the realization that there is something worse than death combined with the modern loss of an alternative way of acting in the world, constitutes a devastating fact unveiled with the rise of Hitler.

This is the fact of evil. But that grossly decontextualizing violence, paradoxically, always occurs in a context that is, in its own insidious way, almost as bad. For the experience of the refugee is not one of relief from the hell that had been their plight before they fled; it is instead its strange consummation in tokens of loss. Refugees attempt to become citizens of their new countries, erasing their prior allegiances, developing new loyalties, second, even third lan-

guages, new selves. Arendt tells the tale of a Mr. Cohn, an exemplar
of the assimilating Jew, who, starting as a German patriot, becomes
in turn—until forced again and again to move on—a Czech patriot, an Austrian patriot, a French patriot. "As long as Mr. Cohn
can't make up his mind to be what he actually is, a Jew, nobody can
foretell all the mad changes he will still have to go through" (271).
The irrevocable fact of Jewish identity, forced upon the refugee,
also illuminates a deep philosophical meaning underlying the idea
of assimilation: "A man who wants to lose his self discovers, indeed,
the possibilities of human existence, which are infinite, as infinite
as is creation. But the recovering of a new personality is as difficult—and as hopeless—as a new creation of the world" (271).

The status of the refugee—this unhappy removal from a life lived
in common with others, thrown into circumstances where friends
are not really friends, but sponsors, where the reasons for being re-
stricted in one's movement shift but one's status as being detached
from others remains a constant—is exactly what I am calling the
experience of loneliness. The refugee is in an incredibly precarious
position.

> If we should start telling the truth that we are nothing but Jews,
> it would mean that we expose ourselves to the fate of human
> beings who, unprotected by any specific law or political con-
> vention, are nothing but human beings. I can hardly imagine
> an attitude more dangerous, since we actually live in a world in
> which human beings as such have ceased to exist for quite a
> while . . . (273)

With the disappearance of the conventions that protect us from
each other, we become nothing but human beings. And to be nothing but human beings, it turns out, means to be nothing at all.
Nothing comes of nothing. Our losses continue to mount. Arendt,
a self-conscious pariah, struggles with her outlaw status, and brings

us the gift of her experience, but it remains to be determined whether that gift is enough. Moreover, it remains to be seen whether the status of refugee is coextensive with the status of the lonely person. The connections between the two are deep and profound. But does the one actually determine the other?

Loneliness and the Vicissitudes of Modernity

Loneliness is the existential realization of a strange fantasy—the loss of self, world, experience, and thought. Arendt's description of such a profound abandonment incites another question concerning the world we now inhabit, one where we always seem to be living in a vestibule of the totalitarian possibility. If that is in fact our possibility now, what is to be done? It at least becomes necessary to describe this condition of loss, the categories through which we continue to live even in their inadequacy, for if this kind of living alone is in fact to be our condition, it is also a condition that still is not the termination point of existence. In other words, imagining that we are lonely, and that we have not yet succumbed to the condition of hard totalitarianism, we may ask ourselves what basic categories may be said to displace those that Arendt presented as becoming lost to us. This is a scenario which may be thought of as fantastic, precisely because it requires us to imagine that we can live in death.

Perhaps the most resolutely pessimistic response to our condition as Arendt imagined it is provided by Giorgio Agamben when he suggests that we are in fact becoming beings whose *nomos* is that of the inhabitants of a camp—that we are on the verge of inhabiting a great zone of indistinction between life and death akin to the experience of the Musselmen of Auschwitz.[9] For Agamben, this is not a ghostly existence; we are the living dead. The categories of living death that would displace those of self, world, experience, and thought seem to be those (inhuman) categories of mass, space, simulation, and logic. The pre-totalitarian moment in the life of a polity—a period of widespread and ordinary loneliness—would then be marked by the displacement of a life of autonomous individuals acting in concert with a massification of social life; the reduction of a common sense of the world into a one-dimensional understanding of neutral space; the displacement of unmediated, face-to-face encounters between humans with ersatz or inauthenticizing encounters with things; and finally, the overcoming of the dialogue of inner thought with the solipsism of objective logic.

Agamben suggests that both Arendt and Foucault lend support to this thesis. And it certainly is true that Arendt's conclusion concerning totalitarianism is bleak, suggesting that humanity has entered a phase of "organized loneliness" encouraged by modern states as a means of increasing the docility of their citizens. In reaching this conclusion, her work fits into a tradition extending back at least to Tocqueville, through Max Weber and most recently, in the American context, Sheldon Wolin. These otherwise diverse thinkers have in common an abiding concern with the ways in which there is a relationship between processes of the pacification of citizens, their subtle subjugation, and the determination of whatever possibility exists for them to be free. In all cases, the struggle for an intellectual purchase that would enable us to understand and embrace freedom becomes arduous—some say impossible. Arendt's argument is saved from complete defeatism by her embrace of what she termed the natal character of humanity, the most general possibility of new beginnings that underlies all human endeavor, and by her sense that a particular form of democratic revolution, American in character, occasionally encourages such beginnings.

In many of her subsequent works, Arendt's concerns about beginnings and the role of promising as expressions of human action oriented toward the future did much to fill in her picture of natality. But the picture, as it develops, still depends on a pre-given sense of the stability of a division between the public and private spheres of life, a highly specific theatricality of political action, and the hierarchical division of human activity into action, work, and labor in order to make possible an ideal realm of pure politics.[10] Unfortunately, sustaining this hierarchy has the potential to do great damage to the human prospects of a majority of those now living, blinding us to the permeability of the barriers that exist between these different realms of life, obscuring our understanding of the ongoing efforts we can make to refashion ourselves out of more complex exercises of imagination. In this sense Arendt did not evade the paradox of the Athenian democracy she so deeply admired, which was built upon the labor of slaves and the subjugation of women. In the end, the very concern that animated her earliest work—an almost tragic sense regarding the fate of humanity—came to be subordinated to the desire to establish the conditions for regaining an imagined realm of autonomous politics.

Probably of more immediate importance is the fact that Arendt's desire to think about the problems of life through the perspective of this hierarchy of activity and division of public and private prevents her from giving appropriate attention to the ongoing struggles we humans undertake at the vital level of the ordinary. And yet it is at this level of experience that we sustain our connections to each other in our most immediate way. This limitation on her political imagination is telling. Our experience of the ordinary gives shape to, as much as it is influenced by, the divisions of life activity she describes. And the ongoing loneliness that becomes absolute under the governance of a totalitarian regime is countered by the (perhaps all too) ephemeral exchanges of democratic communication, even within the shadows of that state. These exchanges may be thought of as composing the dark matter of the life-world, an invisible, immeasurable dimension of freedom that accounts for some of the most profoundly transformative possibilities available to us.

Arendt is hardly alone in seeing a solution to the problem of political existence as being accomplished by the reestablishment and sustenance of a strong separation of the public and private spheres. But whether the political dimension of life is valorized or denigrated by the particular emphasis a thinker may place on aspects of this division, what ends up happening for many of these thinkers is an implicit enunciation of a wish to escape from the debilitating effects of power in order to achieve some sort of sense of peace. In this sense, the desire to preserve an autonomous realm of the political is paradoxically what leads so many in the modern era to seek ways to evade politics—in the end, as Foucault once suggested, going so far as to risk our very existence in the name of strategies designed to put an end to politics once and for all. Indeed, this desire to put an end to politics, undertaken in the name of securing ourselves, may well be the deepest political paradox of our age.

Perhaps we do not need to be so resolutely negative in our thinking. As we imagine new categories that would be more consonant with the range of potential states of being in a lonely world, staying in touch with the negative is important. But this needs to be leavened with the realization that we are *always* living at the end of the world. Our possibilities are defined as much by such endings as by beginnings. So even as there is a quality of living death connected to the terminal experience of loneliness, at the same time we are also presented with the gift, ongoing, of evidence for our continued existence, a potential for living available to us at every moment. In glimpses of Arendt's concept of natality, Cavell's realization of the everyday, Connolly's ethos of pluralization, Foucault's care of self, Thoreau's encouragement to live, Emerson's cheering us on, or any other encouragements of continual life, we may in fact determine how we can think through this *nomos,* to something beyond it, however strongly it presents itself to us as an absolute condition. More banally, proof of the still open possibilities for human existence is quite simply our continued presence on this earth, the fact that you are reading what I am writing, wherever and whoever we may be. That fact may not be enough to see us through, but still . . .

So I want to accept Arendt's argument concerning the fate of the modern self, world, experience, and thought as a provisional and incomplete description of the vicissitudes of modernity. To accept it as more than provisional would be to succumb to a formal pessimism concerning the extent to which experience in general may tutor us and, more specifically, to a substantive despair concerning the prospects of contemporary, degraded democracy. On the other hand, to do less than confront the challenge she presents to us would be to fail to acknowledge the profoundly dangerous political dimension of loneliness, the way we are driven by it to such problematic dead-ends in love and life. My hope is that the weight of different dimensions of experience and their connections to each other—psychological, social, cultural, political—can be reckoned in a such a way as to allow a more robust sense of the meaning of loneliness to emerge.

How are we available to be with each other? How may there be room in our hearts to share our condition with each other, without succumbing to the false optimism of a new communitarian vision of republican virtue or the harsh demands of a liberal individualism that offers no comfort to us imperfect beings or, worst of all, without giving up in the face of our current corporate regime of elite power and massive disenfranchisement? These putatively public problems may be traced back to the problem of our lonely ways of living our lives. It is precisely because of the lonely roots of these public problems that it may be possible that the materials for thinking about our current way of being our selves, materials that may lead us to conceive how we may become something other than our current selves, are, as Emerson once suggested, strewn on the ground before us, readily available to us even as we despair about being able to change our ways. This is to be our question: Can we imagine our selves otherwise than as we are?

Three modes of lonely being dominate our lives in the modern era—having, loving, and grieving. Each mode of being restrains the self in a kind of solitude that turns toward isolation. We learn to be lonely through possession and dispossession, through the experience of loving and the loss of love, which can occur both through processes of growth and separation, and through the deaths of those we love. Each of these modes of being is embedded in habits of everyday life. Each expresses itself through narratives of despair and power, rituals of truth, institutional arrangements. All are entwined with each other, so that the possibility of addressing each separately is not really possible, try as we may.

We all know these stories of loneliness, but each of us must tell the story separately. Of course, these modes of being lonely are not exhaustive of our lonely possibilities, but they still may be thought of as common, quasi-universal experiences of modern life. We tell stories about what it means to possess and be dispossessed, about family dramas of isolation and violence, about the deaths of those whom we love, about the loneliness that ensues from loss. We may learn from these experiences just how lonely we are able to be.

Chapter II

Having

Tragedy . . . is the consequence of man's total compulsion to evaluate himself.

—Arthur Miller

Selling and Being Sold

To be lonely is to be without recourse to others. Yet we wander through life in the presence of other people. How can we be in the presence of others without connecting to them? What kind of experience is it to be with others without communion, connection, or conversation? Hannah Arendt used the term *behavior* to characterize such a way of being in the world. The behavioral self is one whose experience of life is habitual, who responds to the world in conformist terms, who is not *acting,* or *making,* but at best *laboring.* Such a self is diminished in her eyes, an incompletely realized human being. But it may well be that this sort of judgment is the most unhandsome element of her thought; it lends itself to a reactive form of thinking about the ways of ordinary life. For even, or perhaps especially, in our labors we reveal ourselves to be more than laborers. How we attend to each other at these levels, where thought is barely present, where our acts are almost indiscernible, makes a hash of firm distinctions between labor, work, and action.

There is more to the behavioral self than habit, normalization, and the force of labor. Behavior is a story to be told, like all of our stories. The life of the behavioral self is mediated through metaphors of possession. The dimension of our selves that is predominantly behavioral gives expression to the idea that our selves are owned, if not by others, then by ourselves. If it is true that being lonely means that we come to know ourselves in ways that call into question our solidity as human beings, that the world itself disappears over a horizon as others become lost to us, it is true as well that we are also poised on the edge of another precipice. That is, we are constantly enjoined to think about ourselves in relationship to others through terms of possession and dispossession. This compulsion is a consequence of the brute fact of political economy, but also of the less obviously appreciated power of metaphor—we are shaped by the metaphors we live by, even as we shape them. As Emerson writes in "Fate," "The spirit makes its house, but then the house confines the spirit." In thinking about the terms through which we possess and are possessed, we are continuing to think through the practices that have encouraged our ways of being free and that at the same time have imposed limits upon us as we seek new paths of appearance and disappearance.

What is it that we want? Perhaps it is only the acquisition of more of what we have. In our culture—a civilization of consumption if ever there has been one—the lonely self seeks to possess something to call its own, and ends up by confusing that something with itself. The great drive of capital is to turn everything into a commodity, including the self. In this sense, capitalism may be thought of as a symptom of the lonely self. I do not think we can separate the two—they are so conjoined in our epoch. But if the lonely self is in an important sense shaped by the creation of a desire for more, and if this desire in turn gives rise to an anxiety that accompanies the experience of buying and selling, then the anxiety of the lonely self when facing the world of others leads to the deep risk of our selves being bought and sold. Under the spell of the things we own and the things we want, we are able to disappear in new ways, to lose ourselves in our collections, to withdraw into our possessions. We come to look outward from ourselves in new ways, to compare ourselves to others through a standard measure that we ardently hope will convey a new sense of reality to the world, grounded in what we may call the imperatives of behavior, where being is reduced to having—this is, in fact, the core of the etymology of the compound word *be-have*—where our very reality is fundamentally shaped by realty.[1]

What I am trying to suggest is that the ripe ground for the cultivation of a very thin form of the self, the possessed self, is to be found anywhere it is possible to imagine both sovereignty and abjection as flip sides of the same way of being. This phenomenon of power and powerlessness combined is to be found throughout our world in this era of globalization. But when we come upon it in the United States, I think we arrive in a place where that opposition is more starkly presented than it is in many other places, as a consequence of the terms of our settlement, the brutal history of American slavery, and the culture of capitalism. A certain way of being has been encouraged in this culture, and that way of being has created its own ghosts.

I am quite aware that this observation is not news. From at least the seventeenth century, political philosophers have noted that the self that possesses and is possessed plays a determining role in shaping modern life. The capitalist imperative has even (mistakenly) been determined by some of our most important thinkers to be the form that human nature itself takes. We are shaped by the powers of possession, and it is at least true that we struggle to compete in a field of possibility shaped by rules of ownership and its lack. We may even say that our very being is deeply informed by what we *have* and how we are *had*. But though our desires and dreams are shaped by the two sides of this same imperative—it could be the case that dispossession is the dream of the outside of capital—it is also still the case that there is no absolute limit yet formed by capitalism's horizon. Capitalism has a genealogy, just as morality does, just as the self does. And while we may be lacking, we also are shaped by more than lack.

In all the turnings of having and being there have emerged two figures in the culture of capitalism whose stories I wish to explore, two exemplary figures in the history of having. Each of these figures represents a particular form of abjection through the turns of possession, following the pathos of disappearance to different termination points. Yet in the end, both of these figures find that disappearance itself is the signature experience of the lonely self.

First there is the salesman—the one who negotiates the price, delivers the goods. The salesman contributes nothing material to the good of a thing, but juxtaposes things and persons. The salesman is the person, we are told, who gets us to "yes," who finds the bottom line—our ultimate reader of the worth of things. In the work he performs the salesman is a grand logician of capital, arranging the order of the consumption of goods, telling us who and how we are to be as having creatures. In a world of commodification we are what we buy, and the salesman offers us his shallowness, his complete insubstantiality, to mediate our choices. He is a real nowhere man, not of himself, a form of the lonely self sustained by the never quite completion of a final sale.

It is not as though someone could sell things and not live a life, but it is a sign of the times of capitalism that the life of a salesman is lived as something wholly separate from the core of what he does to make a living. Making a living—not the living of a life—is more radically separated for the salesman, perhaps, than for any other kind of modern person. And yet the salesman is more central to modern capitalist culture than any other figure.

It is a source of neither shame nor pride to tell you something more. I am sensitive to the life of the salesman in large part because my father made his career as a life insurance salesman, an agent and manager, a thirty-year employee of the Metropolitan Life Insurance Company. His skills at selling were formidable—he fed and clothed nine children, provided private schooling for all of us, and steered us one and all toward higher education—but those skills at selling were not transferable to home. How could they be? Home life is not supposed to be a realm of buying and selling. Our family's happiness did not depend upon the work my dad did for Metropolitan Life for anything other than the money it assembled. Dad's life was his family, and as I think about the insubstantiality of the salesman, how life is always elsewhere in a special way for such men and women, I imagine what it would mean for him to return home after an evening spent explaining to potential clients why they should purchase a whole life policy from Mother Met (as we used to call his company). Would he think about what he had said, how he had gotten his clients to "yes," or how he had failed? Would his concern for the likely beneficiaries of the clientele keep him awake at night? Or would he have been imagining another life for himself entirely?

No one lives a life without wondering what else you might have done, who else you might have become. But when you are a salesman, is there not an added urgency to the question? This is the pathos of the salesman, his path to disappearance. It is what makes the salesman a figure of discomfort in our culture, someone to be avoided, someone who, because he is uncertain who he is, is thought to be not quite honest, not quite real, not quite right. Ned Ryerson, the brilliantly drawn figure of the insurance salesman in the film *Groundhog Day*, embodies this self-doubt comically, with his rapid-fire question that punctuates every statement he makes: "Am I right or am I right? Right! Right? Right?" Eventually his assertion dissolves into a sort of barking growl, and the salesman becomes like a dogged dog, snapping at his prospective customer.[2]

We detect in the salesman fundamental doubts about ourselves, but we also believe that with his help we will find the means available to us to overcome those doubts. In this sense I sometimes have thought that the salesman is a secular version of clergy, steering us through life, accompanying us on the road to nowhere, pointing us in a particular direction. And thus when we fail, our failure has been his failure as well. "Can't everyone just be happy, dammit?!" was my father's most common exclamation in the face of familial discord and chaos (of which there was plenty). Of course the answer is "No, we can't," but it is the core desire of the salesman for all of us to achieve happiness. The pursuit of happiness becomes the pursuit of goods, or of the security we come to identify with goods. The problem is that the very effort to attain happiness through possession becomes a primary source of unhappiness, intensifying the sense of loss.

The salesman is a figure so thin as to lack substantiality, and his struggle is to be visible. This is not true of my other figure, he who is in constant fear, not of being unable to sell, but of being sold. Not yet owned, but always potentially owned, the free man of the era when chattel slavery had become an institutional possibility for anyone who was designated as black, when other forms of slavery were in the air—this man is the invisible man, the ghostly presence of abjection. He will try to tell us his tale, but always under the guise of a pseudonym. The exploration of this paradox of invisibility is, of course, Ralph Ellison's famous contribution to American thought. Yet Ellison's understanding, as modern and persistent as it is, is preceded by another, even more secretive uncovering, from within the heart of a story that has served as the template for so much of American literature, and that has provided us with the language to imagine something that would eventually be recognized as American culture, Herman Melville's *Moby-Dick*.

There is a problem, at least for me, in thinking about the paradox of visibility and invisibility illuminated by these two figures.

How to put this? Whatever claims of personal experience I may be able to draw upon for having lived with a salesman as my father are not available to me as I try to think about the experience of blackness in a white-dominated culture. Here my intuition and experience desert me, and I must rely instead on reliable witnesses, people who may be able to tell me more about the terror of being placed in a position where one's value is solely determined by the impersonal judgments that flow from an assessment of the color of one's skin. Not having had meaningful experience as a victim of racism myself, hence not having lived with it as anything other than a guilty beneficiary of its poisonous fruits, but observing its persistence into the twenty-first century, I can only imagine the loneliness of racial abjection through the reports of those who could be bought and sold.

Both seller and sold are characters, but I believe they are characters whose existence may allow us to explore in a purer form than usual the existential dilemmas of the lonely self. They are pushed to go to places that are beyond the places where we go in ordinary times, into spaces and moments that may reveal what the limits of existence are for us now. Both seller and sold are present in our present, but they come at it from another angle; they are members, like us, of the America we are always approaching but never quite reaching, striving to become something other than what they are, showing us who we might become, someday, if things fall out the way they often do. They are our advance scouts on the road to nowhere, on the horizon of a new becoming.

The Number-One Man

What happens when disappearance becomes the signature event of one's life? This is the question we are asked to consider in *Death of a Salesman*. Arthur Miller claims of his play that the story "is absurdly simple! It is about a salesman and it's his last day on earth."[3] This last day is by all appearances of no consequence. The plot is simple: Willy Loman fails to drive to Boston, goes to bed, wakes up the next morning, goes into the office and is fired from his job, meets his sons for drinks before dinner, is abandoned by them in the bar, goes home, and kills himself by driving his car into a ditch. There is also a series of failed meetings, misunderstandings, delusional conversations with his wife and children, exhausted reveries, and hallucinatory memories. Willy's last day consists of nothing worth remembering, nothing worth putting together as the meaning of a life. He embraces his death at the end of the second day, believing it will give him worth posthumously. But even in death it is not a final reality that he seeks, but another reality that he tries to evade.

In every move he makes, Willy exposes the black hole at the heart of the possessed self. His sons are strangers to him; he loves his wife but easily betrays her; he sees himself as a friend to his customers, but they do not consider him a friend. His one true friend is someone he cannot stand. He imagines that he would be happy if the refrigerator were a better brand, if his house wasn't hemmed in by other buildings, if his son Biff had gone to college, if his boss would let him sell out of the headquarters, if the mortgage was paid, if his insurance payment was met, if his car was repaired. But Willy's line is over; he is dreaming only of the past. He is at a place in life where his use has ended.

As is true for Lear, the tragedy of Willy's present is shaped by his failure to be present. But unlike Lear, his absence is plotted through a series of fragmented incursions of the past upon his present, until his very presence in the present is lost to him. This dynamic of remembrance is a key to understanding Willy's dilemma—how is one to remember the past when to do so is to force oneself to be faced with the consequences of the past's power to shape the unhappy present? Each moment in the play is imbued with regret as the characters address their mistakes; their accounting adds up to lives of meaningless wandering through the detritus of used and worn-out objects. But this is not a Marxist critique of capitalism. Miller is struggling to express another thought, in which the imperative of acquisition is tied to the false memory of a pastoral way of life. This dream of America is far different from the idea of the American dream.

Miller's play was once considered by some to be a masterpiece of social realism, but what is most remarkable about it is its dreamlike quality, as the past is dramatically blended into and comes to determine the tragic present. Miller knew that he would be juxtaposing past and present in an unprecedented way, and the staging was to be crucial to realizing this vision of past and present commingling. Radical in design, the stage set was composed of three floating platforms and an empty space, permitting movement between past and present through slight lighting changes and subtle positioning of furniture. This was not the film technique of flashback; the intent was instead to show the past in the present, to make the power of the past at key moments intrude not only upon Willy but, through Willy's incoherent but compelling descriptive powers, to his sons, his wife, his boss, and his neighbor. (The conflation of past and present occurs early in the first act, when Willy misremembers having opened the windshield of his automobile [DS, 7–8].) The living past surges into the present, fusing the two in Willy's consciousness, confusing his wife, sons, and neighbors. This fusing, this confusion, constitutes Miller's account of this life—the fullness of it, the bleakness of it, *this* life in its completion. Turning this life upon itself, making its pivotal events elements of the present, marks Willy's death as a profound fulfillment of an unfulfilled life, flashing before our eyes.

Miller's rendering is of a death that, like all deaths, marks the completion of a life. But his play presents a particular understanding of how we are to imagine our lives in their completion. The folds of time in the play suggest a theory of time itself. Past and present are interwoven to show how this particular person has become who he is through processes of denial, suppression, and delusion, but also of action, hope, and humor. This is a way of capturing time, allowing us to gain a more intimate knowledge of these characters, as though we have come to know them through the duration of their lives.

The folding of past into present is ubiquitous in this play. There is not a major character in the play who does not experience the presence of the past as a marker of great significance for themselves. Everyone in the Loman family is acquainted with the unspiraling of a common past, its culmination in the moment. In this way, Willy Loman's final day on earth becomes a dreamscape of accomplishment and failure against which the other people in his life will eventually need to give accounts of themselves as well. What is Happy's shallowness about? Where does Biff's self-destructiveness come from? Why is Linda so forgiving? We are given an entry into their lives by way of these juxtapositions of the past to the present which cumulatively reveal the complex presence of the past, the present revealing itself as a fugitive fusion of encounters between the now and the then, family secrets made known by the ghostly presence of former selves whose dreams have gone wrong.

The struggle with dreams—when to embrace them, how to escape them—is in fact a major motif of the play, one that becomes increasingly dominant as the play moves forward. When we reach the conclusion, the Requiem following Act Two, the dream is an explicit theme.

> BIFF: He had the wrong dreams. All, all, wrong.
> HAPPY [*almost ready to fight* BIFF]: Don't say that.
> BIFF: He never knew who he was.
> CHARLEY [stopping HAPPY's movement and reply. To BIFF]:
> Nobody dast blame this man. You don't understand.
> Willy was a salesman. And for a salesman there is no rock
> bottom to the life. He don't put a bolt on a nut, he don't

tell you the law or give you medicine. He's a man way out
there in the blue, riding on a smile and shoeshine. And
when they start not smiling back—that's an earthquake.
And then you get yourself a couple spots on your hat, and
you're finished. Nobody dast blame this man. A salesman
has got to dream, boy. It comes with the territory.

BIFF: Charley, the man didn't know who he was.

HAPPY [*infuriated*]: Don't say that!

BIFF: Why don't you come with me, Happy?

HAPPY: I'm not licked that easily. I'm staying right in this
city, and I'm gonna beat this racket! [*He looks at* BIFF, *his
chin set.*] The Loman Brothers!

BIFF: I know who I am, kid.

HAPPY: All right, boy. I'm gonna show you and everybody
else that Willy Loman did not die in vain. He had a good
dream. It's the only dream you can have—to come out
number-one man. He fought it out here, and this is where
I'm gonna win it for him. (DS, 111)

These men have defined themselves for and against a particular
dream, what Happy describes as coming out as the number-one
man. It is no accident that Willy's name, Loman, is a direct description of his status. As opposed to number one, he is the low man.
That he is so measured is the core of the tragedy of his life. But how
can someone measure up when, as Happy claims, to be number-
one man is the *only* dream you can have? Charley defends Willy; he
has an understanding of Willy's fall, the earthquake of failure coming when the customers stop smiling back. "And then you get yourself a couple spots on your hat, and you're finished," he says. The
clothes make the man, the appearance is all, and it is foolish to
think otherwise. There is no authenticity here, nothing but the representation of the self as a success that is waiting to happen, that has
happened, that will forever be happening. Recognition fuses with

possession—sales are the measure of a man, there is no anchor to the life, only a constant comparison.

This nominal form of measurement is nihilistic, a straightforward fulfillment of the nihilism of capital, but also more specifically the nihilism of possessive individualism. To strive to achieve the dream of being number one when there is never a number one in the vacated throne of power is to strive toward nothingness in the name of fulfillment. To reach this place could only mean the total absorption of the self into a complete and priceless possession. This logic parallels Thomas Hobbes's thought that we could act in unison in the absence of God only through a strict adherence to the mechanical laws of nature, giving up our desire for everything, handing over all power, including that of life and death, to a sovereign being in exchange for the peace which would lead us to commodious living, the possession of things. Politically speaking, the number-one man is he who has absorbed all others into himself and is perfect in his stillness, in his holding of the power of all within himself. He allows the rest of us to be, since we are a part of him. And we will be prosperous to the extent that we keep still as well. Nobody moves, nobody gets hurt.

Yet we know that commodious living offers no peace, that our confinement in the place of powerlessness leads us to futile striving or an embrace of nothingness. In the face of the nihilism of number one, Biff's claim that he knows who he is—nothing—is thus the best possible response, a response that may free him from the demands of this form of accounting. But his knowledge is bought at another price: a severe accounting of himself that permits no more dreams of the future.

To account for themselves is the task that all of these characters face. But to give an account of oneself, to question the terms of one's existence, in a culture of self-possession is paradoxical, because the measures each person is able to bring to bear in order to investigate the state of his or her self reduce the worth of each to a price.

To give an account of oneself is to be thrust into the infernal machine of evaluation, and evaluation is a form of ownership. As Hobbes put it, "A man's price is his worth."[4]

It is not as though these people are unaware of their struggle in this regard. In the first act of *Death of a Salesman,* Linda tries to put a rock bottom to Willy's life: "He's a human being, and a terrible thing is happening to him. So attention must be paid. He's not to be allowed to fall into his grave like an old dog. Attention, attention must finally be paid to such a person" (DS, 40). And yet Willy is not noticed, attention isn't paid, no one shows up at his funeral, his only freedom is in his death. The anchor does not hold. Why is there no bottom, no grounding? If it is only the nihilism of an accounting that does not permit us to find ourselves, then we simply must forswear that way of life. But there is more to it than that.

The avoidance of love and the shame of the father permeate this play as much as they do *The Tragedy of King Lear.* Yet here the division of the estate is not in question so much as the recuperation of a love that has been lost through a failure to measure up to the demands of success, that is, to become number one, to achieve the form of power most available in a system where sovereignty has been divided and sold off. This is the power of possession, of goods, but finally of oneself. The failure to achieve this state is most fully pronounced in the relationship of Willy to Biff. The secret of their relationship—Biff's discovery of his father's cheating on his mother, which leads him to punish his father by destroying his own opportunity to go to college—is less important for that discovery than for the revelation concerning the hollowness of Willy's life ("I was lonely, I was terribly lonely," he confesses to Biff [DS, 95]). In the replaying of this moment, Biff has come to his father to tell him that he has failed a course and cannot graduate. The course he has failed is math—he has failed to learn to calculate, to count. This failure leads Biff out of the life that Willy has imagined for him, and yet he does not find his way forward. In the present of the play,

Biff is still stuck, a failure at thirty-four, unable to act. But Willy, unable to understand Biff's failure, still imagines that Biff is ready to become a success, that he is one interview away from the break he needs. When Biff tells him that there is no interview, that he is "a bum," that he is leaving, the scene is set for their mutual confessions of love and denial.

This final scene of love and love's denial inverts the opening scene of *Lear*. In *Death* the mother is present; in *Lear* the mother is missing. In *Death* the oldest son must profess his love; in *Lear* it is the youngest daughter. In *Lear* the father initiates the confrontation; in *Death,* the son. In *Lear* the father's estate is being divided after signs of love; in *Death* an inheritance is to be provided after the father's death. Yet the themes of love and its avoidance are similar, if posed from a different position, from the status of those whose loss is not incipient but constant, who can only imagine the fulfillment of their dreams in an indefinite and never to be realized future.

The scene is set when Biff and Happy return from dinner, after having abandoned their father for the evening. Biff has concluded that he must leave and not return. He wants to speak to his father. His mother doesn't want him to go near Willy, accusing him of not caring whether Willy lives or dies. She calls Biff a louse. He responds, "Now you hit it on the nose! . . . The scum of the earth, and you're looking at him!" (DS, 99). This is Biff's self-realization, what he wants to share with his father—the fact that he is a failure, not simply as a deal maker, but as a human being. He has left his father "babbling in a toilet" (DS, 98). He is worthless, but it is his revelation of his worthlessness that is to free him from the bondage of being Willy Loman's son.

Biff ignores his mother and goes to the garden, where his father is trying to plant seeds in the darkness of the night. (He goes to his father immediately after Willy has finished his conversation with his dead brother, Ben, concerning the idea of an inheritance in the form of a $20,000 life insurance payment for his sons. Willy worries that the company won't pay, but he also worries that he won't be brave enough to kill himself.) In this garden—there is a faint echo of Gethsemane in the scene—Biff explains to his father that he can't explain himself to him: "Today I realized something about myself and I tried to explain it to you and I—I think I'm just not smart enough to make any sense out of it for you. To hell with whose fault it is or anything like that" (DS, 101–102). This last failure, a failure to explain, to be understood, places Biff in the tradition established by Cordelia, who cannot put her heart into her mouth. For Biff this is a moment of freedom, of being able to let go, to begin to forgive himself for who he has become. It is the possibility of a kind of redemption.

And yet Biff, not unlike Cordelia, still seeks his father's blessing. He invites Willy to go into the house to tell Linda what has transpired. Willy, weighed down by the guilt of his decision to kill himself, doesn't want to see her. He is nervous and ashamed, and his shame turns quickly into rage. When they reenter the house, he ignores his son as Biff explains to Linda what has happened. She agrees that it is for the best that Biff leave, because he and Willy will "just never get along" (DS, 102). Willy refuses to shake Biff's hand, still insisting that Biff could keep his appointment, retrieve a lost opportunity, and make good with the businessman whose pen Biff has robbed. Willy's blindness here initiates a great unraveling.

> BIFF [*gently*]: Dad, you're never going to see what I am, so
> what's the use of arguing? If I strike oil I'll send you a
> check. Meantime forget I'm alive.
> WILLY [*to* LINDA]: Spite, see?
> BIFF: Shake hands, Dad.
> WILLY: Not my hand.

BIFF: I was hoping not to go this way.

WILLY: Well, this is the way you're going. Good-bye.

[BIFF *looks at him a moment, then turns sharply and goes to the stairs.*]

WILLY [*stops him with*]: May you rot in hell if you leave this house!

BIFF [*turning*]: Exactly what is it that you want from me?

WILLY: I want you to know, on the train, in the mountains, in the valleys, wherever you go, that you cut down your life for spite!

BIFF: No, no.

WILLY: Spite, spite, is the word of your undoing! And when you're down and out, remember what did it. When you're rotting somewhere beside the railroad tracks, remember and don't you dare blame it on me!

BIFF: I'm not blaming it on you!

WILLY: I won't take the rap for this, you hear? (DS, 103)

Here the themes of recognition and love are inverted. Willy cannot see that Biff is offering to leave home for good out of his sense of worthlessness, for to recognize this would be to challenge his cherished illusions concerning how he has loved and raised his sons. Lear sought the counterfeit love of Regan and Goneril so as to avoid the reality of Cordelia's love, a love worthy of him but shameful to him. Willy tries to avoid responsibility for his son's failure so as not to have to look at what his own life has been, which would make him ashamed. For if Biff is worthless, so is Willy. Hence, Willy must reread Biff's failure as an act of spite, a repudiation of Willy rather than a fulfillment of his legacy. He rejects blame, even as his memories accuse him of having failed his sons.

For Willy to accuse Biff of being spiteful is similar to the false charge that Lear raises against Cordelia of not loving him. It is as though Willy seeks his own form of counterfeit love, a love that would assure him that he has loved his sons properly, has given them a love that will allow them to go forth in life and become number-one men. Biff is trying to demonstrate the opposite of spite, just as Cordelia is trying to show her true love, not a counterfeit love, as a way of being loyal to her father. It is a true love that inspires Biff's desire to leave his father. How he demonstrates this love constitutes the final paradox of the play. In the face of the accusation of spite, Biff acts spitefully, confronting Willy with a rubber hose that was to be the instrument of Willy's suicide by suffocation, declaring that there will be no pity for Willy. Willy repeats the charge of spite, and Biff responds: "No, you're going to hear the truth—what you are and what I am!" (DS, 104). Biff's desire to speak the truth is based on his sense that his acknowledgment of the truth will lead him to a better place than where he is. But he has to get past Willy's falsehood to get there. "I never got anywhere because you blew me so full of hot air I could never stand taking orders from anybody! That's whose fault it is! . . . What am I doing in an office, making a contemptuous, begging fool of myself, when all I want is out there, waiting for me the minute I say I know who I am!" (DS, 105). This hot air is poison to Biff, as would be the gas that the rubber hose would deliver to Willy. Biff rejects such a suicide for himself as he challenges Willy to acknowledge what he has so far hidden from everyone—his own sense of worthlessness, his failure in the face of the endless striving to be number one.

Willy refuses to shake Biff's hand. Is his refusal merely spite, or is it possible that Willy, like Lear, realizes that his hand stinks of mortality? At this pivotal moment Willy is unable to *see* Biff. "Dad," Biff says, "you are never going to see who I am." Willy is blinded by his shame, which emerges as a false pride, and by his fear, which is that he will be discovered in his shame to have not loved his son well enough, to have been simply too weak to love him. "I won't

take the rap for this, you hear?" he cries. The rap for what? For
Biff's failure, for his loss, for his refusal to properly abdicate? What
would abdication look like for this low man?

Biff's truth is simple and final: "I'm a dime a dozen and so are
you!" (DS, 105). In the face of Willy's protest—"I am not a dime a
dozen! I am Willy Loman and you are Biff Loman!"—Biff asserts
his worthlessness. His claim culminates in an exhausted statement
of his truth.

> BIFF [*at the peak of his fury*]: Pop, I'm nothing! I'm nothing,
> Pop. Can't you understand that? There's no spite in it any
> more. I'm just what I am, that's all.
> [BIFF's *fury has spent itself, and he breaks down, sobbing,*
> *holding on to* WILLY, *who dumbly fumbles for* BIFF's *face.*]
> (DS, 106)

Nothing comes of nothing, says Lear, setting off a tragedy in his
insistence that false love be spoken to him. Biff responds to Willy's
demand that he assert himself as a somebody with the truth of his
worthlessness, the fact that he is nothing. This statement is beyond
spite; it comes from a desire to assess and spare the father of his responsibility for the condition of the son. For the father to accept
the forgiveness of the son is unbearable. That is the core of Willy's
shame.

Even Willy's response to Biff's breakdown, to his tears, with
a new realization, that Biff loves him after all, entails an illusion, the illusion that will lead to his death. After Biff, exhausted
by his struggle, goes to bed, Willy is left to ponder what he has
witnessed.

> WILLY: Oh, Biff! [*Staring wildly*] He cried! Cried to me. [*He*
> *is choking with love, and now cries out his promise.*] That
> boy—that boy is going to be magnificent! (DS, 106)

But Biff isn't magnificent. He is a drifter, a nothing, a person haunted by the failure of his father, inheriting his father's stink of failure. Nevertheless, Willy's dead brother Ben reappears before Willy, reaffirms his false judgment—"Yes, outstanding, with twenty thousand behind him"—and Willy's course is set. Willy kills himself so that his family may collect the insurance money and so that his sons may become the men they are meant to be. Biff and Happy, he imagines, can now become the successful men that he has always pictured them being. But they won't. A key element in the tragedy of *Death of a Salesman* is the frustration of the life ambitions of Happy and Biff, who are unable to become who they want to be. They are failures by comparison to their father's deluded sense of who they are and who they may become. Willy sees a magnificence in Biff—more so than in Happy, who, having more fully bought into the delusional sense of success, has nothing to offer his father in the way of real love other than more of the same illusions that Willy has been plying for years.

Through his focus on the power of a commingled past and present, Miller re-creates a sense of the difficult struggle, as Biff suggests, to know oneself. For Biff, self-realization is the result of disillusionment, a recognition of his failure to measure up. Biff reverts to a pastoral dream—a wish to live under the skies of the west, to work with his hands. Happy will try to redeem his father's memory by beating "the racket," conning his way into success, still imagining that he may somehow become number one. But there is no number one to become. Neither of the sons will become a whole man; both will be fragments of the fragmented Willy, the man torn asunder by his dreams of possession. It is a fulfillment of the prophecy to be found in what is, if read from a particular angle, one of the bleakest lines in all of Emerson's writings: "Dream delivers us to dream, and there is no end to illusion."

In the final lines of the play, Linda, speaking to Willy's grave, places a decisive imprint upon the tragedy of possession. "I made the last payment on the house today. Today, dear. And there'll be nobody home. [*A sob rises in her throat.*] We're free and clear. [*Sobbing more fully released.*] We're free. [BIFF *comes slowly toward her.*] We're free . . . We're free . . ."(DS, 112). That Willy's freedom coincides with his death might be thought of as heavy-handed irony. But it is only the result of a life in which the economy of being requires one to inhabit a house, not in fulfillment of a pastoral vision, but as someone who is purchasing himself—becoming through possessing one's self. Under these conditions, to become free is to own oneself, to be clear of the state of debt, to overcome one's status as beholden to others, in short, to be alone. This is the account of one's life, paid in full. A payment in full is something that is hard to believe in, but it is the faith we are asked to hold in these days of late capitalism.

One might say that the self who owns himself is death-bound. But so are we all, death-bound, that is. From one perspective, total possession is only a form of dispossession, one that involves us in the problem of existence in a way that distracts us from accounting for our selves. Thus we come full circle, to a point where our freedom is bought at the price of our subjection. Is there any other way?

In his final essay, a reflection on the immanence of being, Gilles Deleuze put the problem of our connection to existence this way: "It may be that to believe in this world, in this life, has become our most difficult task, the task of a mode of existence to be discovered on our plane of immanence today."[5] This idea, the idea of "a life," is densely complex, almost impossible for any single mind to grasp. Deleuze writes, "We will say of pure immanence that it is A LIFE, and nothing else. It is not immanence to life, but the immanent that is in nothing is itself a life. A life is the immanence of immanence, absolute immanence: it is complete power, complete bliss" (27). The phrase "the immanent that is in nothing is itself a life" bespeaks the death that awaits us all, each and every one of us, and the realization that until that moment we cannot provide a full assessment of who we are. In this realization there is as much hope as despair, even for the self who has had as his primary experience the pathos of disappearance. The nothings of Lear are revisited in the immanence of immanence. When Willy asks his (dead) brother Ben, "Does it take more guts to stand here the rest of my life ringing up a zero?" (DS, 100), he is ready to face nothingness. When Biff claims he is nothing, he is ready to disappear in yet another way, to go west. In the comings and goings of a life, we face this problem of nothingness. The lonely self knows this nothingness. But what the self knows of it is still not the final lesson of being alone.

Pip and Ishmael

While it may be true that we cannot provide an adequate measure of our possession that will evade the entanglements of nothing, it does not follow that there is no difference between having and being had. The varieties of political and economic experience that involve us in the world of ownership and being owned present us with different lines of flight, other ways of figuring our experiences in terms of violence, harm, and other forms of loss. When we consider slavery, for instance, we know it as the opposite of ownership, but this does not mean it has equal weight to ownership. Consider Herman Melville's *Moby-Dick*.

Moby-Dick is a mountainous book about the sea, an American book of revelation. It represents a world, or worlds, that may be interpreted to infinite degrees, and have been. Since the novel's rehabilitation by F. O. Matthiessen in the first part of the twentieth century, a literary industry has grown to explore its fathomless depths. Journals devoted to Melville seem as much occupied with this one book as with all the rest of his amazing oeuvre put together. Hershel Parker hinges his massive life of Melville around the gestation and publication of *Moby-Dick*. Charles Olson assumes that the study of it is the most meaningful study of Melville (a man who, he claims, and I must agree, was later ruined by his reconversion to Christianity), and it is also Olson who provides the poetry to render future studies of the book weak by comparison. C. L. R. James has made it the quintessential artistic representation of the impossible politics of American racialism. It has been made into film, into opera, and into a Laurie Anderson performance piece. It has been borrowed by all forms of popular culture so ubiquitously that its characters have become a shorthand for specific forms of madness, a fit echoing of Melville's own use of the master Shakespeare's characters. The conflation of Melville the author with the narrator of the story—call him Ishmael (for now)—has encouraged psychoanalytic studies of him, perhaps most prominently Michael Rogin's densely layered argument concerning the family fortune of the Melville clan and the political economy of a country on the brink and in the aftermath of civil war. The influence of the book on one of Melville's own descendants has been so pronounced that he has named himself Moby, and has created ambient music reminiscent of the ocean. It is, in other words, a book to be reckoned with by anyone who wants to think about American experience.

Among its many themes, *Moby-Dick* is a book about loneliness— the loneliness of Ahab, but for me, above all, the loneliness of two of its lesser characters: first, whoever he is who says "Call me Ishmael" and narrates this novel, and second, the cabin boy who is abandoned at sea and goes mad, Pip.

Who is Ishmael? For me, this is the most important question to ask if we are to think about this book in reference to the lonely self. In a way that parallels Judith Butler's concern with the "I" who is to act ethically, the "who" of this question centers our thinking about the ends of loneliness—is there a "who" to whom we may repair, an identity that is able to settle us, a place for our placelessness, a home in the world for the lonely? In the end such a question is a metaphysical one, but its catastrophic irresolution in *Moby-Dick* shows us to be the inheritors of all that has followed from its asking. I am also interested in Pip because his experience forms a part of that inheritance. Pip is the figure who shadows Ishmael. As another member of Ahab's crew, the cook's assistant, Pip is privy to the secret knowledge of the deepest thought-diver whose own secrets are hopelessly entangled with this question, and whose claims on an answer to the question lead us to think again about the circumstances in which we find our selves as lonely beings.

In a recent study of *Moby-Dick,* Eyal Peretz also asks "Who is Ishmael?" and presents his own, startlingly original answers.

> *Moby-Dick* is the narrative of Ishmael, the single survivor and sole witness to a horrendous disaster at sea in which all his friends were killed and brought to an early, stoneless and unmarked grave. As if wanting to share his friends' destiny, he has left his given name at sea and has adopted the Biblical name Ishmael, thus indicating his abandonment and loss. From now on he wishes to be called Ishmael and not by his given name, which remains forever unknown. The story we are about to hear is his testimony, and it is the testimony of a survivor.[6]

Yet this is not all. Peretz notes that Ishmael is a schoolteacher, a depressed person, and that he is drawn to the sea by a strange attraction to the whale itself, this time choosing a whaler as his boat. Moreover, he is anonymous for reasons that touch deeply on the tale that Melville is trying to tell.

"Call me Ishmael." So he addresses the reader. And then he tells a tale. But, Peretz asks us, his readers, what is the tale Ishmael is seeking to tell? Here things begin to get complicated, for the tale is told by someone who is employing a kind of "splitting" address, a narrative where the seaman's yarn is joined to a testimony concerning a disaster, where fable is joined to witnessing. We readers are

encouraged to believe this story, to accept its reality while knowing
of its fabulous character. Monstrous fable is joined to what Ishmael
insists is independent testimony in order to establish the great truth
of the story (37). This ambiguous structure of address, Peretz tells
us, ought to force us to reconsider the meaning of those opening
words: "The opening thus says: either my name is Ishmael and you
should call me by my name; or this is not my given name, but one
called for by the conventions of fiction; or it is my name, carefully
chosen, and in order to explain why I chose it I have to tell you my
life's story; or, since I am an abandoned human, and feel like a dis-
owned son, I call upon you, the readers, to adopt me and call me by
this name so that I won't be alone any more" (39). (This last suggestion also implies that we readers form a lost tribe, that *we* are dis-
owned and abandoned, and that we are seeking some form of redemption by listening to the narrator of this book.)

Peretz moves on to consider how this complex form of address
precludes the likelihood of final meanings, and hence to consider
how this novel leads readers from questions of meaning to questions concerning the relationship of power to authority. What is
launched with Ishmael's desire to go to sea is a series of crises of authority in which the story of the whale as "the white event" overwhelms and interrupts any attempt to reassemble prior meanings.
The whale enables revolutions, the sort of transformations where
nothing will remain the same, but at a cost that will be experienced
by the survivor of the encounter as a shattering of his identity. So
we may call him Ishmael, but that begs the question of who he is
and who he has been. Thus Ishmael's injunction to call him by that
name may itself be understood as a demand or plea that we help
him evade the ghost of his former self.

The possibilities outlined by Peretz advance our understanding
of *Moby-Dick* substantially. But one path is left partly unexplored
by him, a path that opens a different perspective on the fact of shattered identity and its role in the unfolding of a sense of self. This

perspective is intimately connected to the loneliness of the protagonist of the novel. Where to begin? We may note that Ishmael's occupation of schoolteacher gives him special powers to impart lessons of the sea, both factual and moral, to those who choose to
listen to him. (Peretz, later in his analysis, discusses at length Ishmael's attempts to provide pedagogic authority for the tale he witnesses.) In this sense Ishmael could also be imagined as the "metaphysical professor" who accompanies in thought all those who gaze
out to sea (C1).[7] If it is to be Ishmael's life story that is told, though,
it is one that is strangely abridged, for we know very little of him
when we are introduced to him, and nothing of his past experience
other than as a country schoolmaster who has had a rough transition in becoming a seaman. So we are left to sort out those clues we
are given—in this instance, his indirect and perhaps satirical claim
to be a metaphysical professor.

In the same passage where we learn of Ishmael's prior vocation,
he gestures toward a distinguished family tree, commenting on how
hard it is for some to adjust to the lowly status of seaman. "It
touches one's sense of honor, particularly if you come of an old es-
tablished family in the land, the Van Rensselaers, or Randolphs, or
Hardicanutes" (C1).[8] The Van Rensselaers were a distinguished
family, while Hardicanute was a Swedish king, but it is the reference to the Randolphs that is of particular interest. The Randolph
family was one of the oldest and most distinguished of Virginia
families, the family of Thomas Jefferson, which built its fortune
from the labor of its slaves. To imagine oneself a Randolph suggests
that one is a slaveholder. So Ishmael may come from a distinguished
family. But the slippery language suggests that he may not. Moreover, in the very next paragraph he also asks, "Who ain't a slave?"

Another clue. Peretz mentions the fact of Ishmael's name. In the
Bible Ishmael was the first-born son of Abraham, conceived not
with Sarah, his wife, but with Hagar, his slave. When in her barren
years Sarah conceived Isaac, Ishmael and Hagar were sent into ex-

ile. For Peretz, the connotations of banishment and abandonment loom large in this name. Moreover, etymologically, the word "Ishmael" means "God will hear" (36–37). In this sense, the name incorporates the notion of call or address. Peretz emphasizes the excess of meaning to be found in any call, that is, the way a call overrides the meaning contained in it by means of its very form. He writes, "It is as if language is first of all an address and only secondarily a statement of meaning" (39). It is as if, as Giambattista Vico insisted in his *New Science,* all language is first sung, and only later spoken. "Call me Ishmael" thus could be read as: "Call me a call," and as an imperative: "Call this call," "Sing me my song," or "You must sing with me this song." In these words the character of Ishmael anticipates the song of Whitman, but the song is of the disaster, sung by the entire crew.

The call is also a calling, a desire for a vocation: Ishmael goes to sea in a direct attempt to shake off one self and assume another through the vocational acceptance of a calling. The story that is his to tell is the story of his acceptance of the vocation of seaman, of sojourner to the sea. But while he will tell us this tale, it is not one of redemption, even as it assumes the form of a conversion from one form of life to another. The conversion itself will assume the most complicated and devilish form, for what is to be born again is not a soul redeemed, nor, despite the inner turn it takes, a self-reliant self. Another way of putting the matter is to ask the question: Ishmael becomes a seaman, but what was he before? And yet another question: when did he become a seaman? When is Ishmael's moment of conversion?

"God will hear." What will he hear? It is a peculiarity of the novel that upon the departure of the *Pequod* to sea Ishmael seems to disappear, or at least to fade, into the role of the narrator of events. Sometimes the events to which he is witness seem impossible for him to have seen. Occasionally he is an actor in the tale that he narrates. This too is a clue. Among the curiosities of this book, the place of Ishmael as a witnessing narrator is especially curious. First, there is the question of Melville's authorial license: Melville seems to place Ishmael as a witness to crucial scenes throughout the novel, allows him to hear the spoken thoughts of other characters, makes him a seemingly constant presence at the key turns of plot and conversation. Of course, how else is one to tell the tale? We may imagine that within the confines of such a Patagonian crew there is an infinite number of stories to be told, and we may even imagine that Ishmael has witnessed only one iteration of the story. But what happens if we were to press the point, namely that this person we are to call Ishmael is, as Peretz reminds us, *witnessing* events, providing testimony? In that case the omnipresent narrator is *not* a possibility. So we must ask, *how* is it that Ishmael is present at certain scenes that only a witness could describe?

This question concerning the staging of the drama of *Moby-Dick* turns out to be crucial. When we reflect on the confined geography of the *Pequod,* it is clear that for certain of the scenes Ishmael records he would in fact need to be in or near the captain's quarters or the quarterdeck to witness them. For instance, though it would be easy enough to reconstruct the hierarchy of the cabin table without being present, the specific details of the presentation of food and the conversation of the mates and harpooners, as well as the details concerning Dough-Boy, the steward, would need to be provided by an eyewitness (C34). (To suggest that Ishmael might have asked some of the diners what they did at the dinner table is not credible. He is, after all, a *witness,* not a journalist.)

As another instance of Ishmael's mysterious witnessing, we might ask who is present during the conversation between Ahab and Stubb (C29). This is the moment when Ahab is restlessly walking the deck in the middle of the night. Stubb "came up from below" to request that Ahab muffle the noise of his peg-leg with some wadding. The famous confrontation—Ahab calls Stubb a dog ("Down dog, and kennel!")—is told from the perspective of a third party.

Who is this witness? In yet another example, the crucial confrontation between Starbuck and Ahab occurs in the cabin, also requiring
a witness (C109). And finally, we have the startling conversation
between Ahab and Pip in the confines of the captain's cabin. Who
could possibly be witnessing this conversation? (C129).

All of these conversations occur either in the captain's cabin, in
the main cabin, or on the quarterdeck immediately above those
cabins and the mates' quarters. These quarters are in the stern of
the ship, which also contains the captain's hold, from whence
emerged Ahab's secret team on the day of the first lowering (C48).
Moreover, the aft compartment is where the harpooners are lodged,
as opposed to the men at sea (C33). The aft portion of the ship is
also the location of the ship's galley, the place where Pippin, or Pip,
could be found, the person whom Ishmael describes as being the
most insignificant member of the crew, but the one to whom something most significant happens (C93).

Pip is in fact depicted as being the least of the sailors aboard the
Pequod, the most isolated of that crew of isolatoes, tragically gone
mad after he floats for too many hours upon an open sea with no
hope of rescue. Ishmael tells us that prior to his abandonment Pip
was bright and tenderhearted and young, that he hailed from Connecticut, that he was a tambourine player and a free man. On the
Pequod he is a ship-keeper, that is, one who is assigned not to work
the boats, but to assist the cook and perform other menial chores.
But he is assigned as a replacement rower on the second mate
Stubb's whale boat, a position Pip takes with reluctance, since he is
terrified of whales. On his second trip out he entangles himself in
the line, causing it to be cut and hence for Stubb to lose a whale.
After that first mishap Stubb tells Pip, "Stick to the boat, Pip, or by
the Lord, I wont pick you up if you jump; mind that. We can't afford to lose whales by the likes of you; a whale would sell for thirty
times what you would, Pip, in Alabama" (C93). This threat to Pip's

freedom, while satirical on Stubb's part, is frightening to Pip, since he appreciates what Stubb does not—that any black man is compelled to think this thought in anticipation of the Congressional passage of the Fugitive Slave Act, and as an everyday imagining of the horror of the ongoing possibility of becoming a slave.

Pip is abandoned at sea after being assessed as having a worth that is precisely one-thirtieth the value of a whale. This observation is the great catalyst for the subsequent shattering of his mind. Stubb's enunciation of the power of capital to reckon worth underlines the all-too-present potential for Pip's descent into chattel, the possibility of his being placed on shore in a place like Alabama as opposed to his native Connecticut. Like all crew members, Pip's worth is determined by his "lay." In a famous scene, Ishmael undergoes a protracted bargaining session with the owners of the *Pequod* in "The Ship" concerning the lay he is to receive for the voyage, a comical passage concerning the worth of a man (C16). Prepared to sell his services, Pip, like the other sailors, must negotiate his value as a portion of the profit and agree to be paid that amount for the length of his passage on the whaling boat. Given the absolute discipline of the ship (a theme Melville often returns to in his novels), Pip essentially sells himself for the duration of the voyage. Thus he may imagine that, if he is already owned, nothing is to prevent him from being sold, just as Stubb suggests.

Ishmael describes Pip's first fate, his descent into madness after falling out of Stubb's boat, as a consequence of his belief that he has been truly and totally abandoned, just as Stubb had warned that he would be.

> By the merest chance the ship had at last rescued him; but from that hour the negro went about the deck an idiot; such, at least, they said he was. The sea had jeeringly kept his finite body up, but drowned the infinite of his soul. Not drowned entirely,

though. Rather, carried down alive to wondrous depths, where
strange shapes of the unwarped primal world glided to and fro
before his passive eyes; and the miser-merman, Wisdom, revealed his hoarded heaps; and among the joyous, heartless, ever-
juvenile eternities, Pip saw the multitudinous, God-omnipres-
ent, coral insects, that out of the firmament of waters heaved
the colossal orbs. He saw God's foot upon the treadle of the
loom, and spoke it; and therefore his shipmates called him mad.
So man's insanity is heaven's sense; and wondering from all
mortal reason; man comes at last to that celestial thought,
which to reason, is absurd and frantic; and weal or woe, feels
then uncompromised, indifferent as his God. (C93)

So when Pip falls from the boat a second time he knows himself to
be lost—even though it turns out that his abandonment is not a
deliberate act by Stubb, but a tragic oversight. And so, it seems, is
his descent into madness. But Pip's self-knowledge and self-loss, we
come to learn, are both a part of a complicated mystery.

Ishmael's portrait of Pip emphasizes, prior to his abandonment,
his pleasant, genial, jolly brightness. Yet Ishmael also insists on Pip's
brilliance, his exemplary character, his depth as a human being. In
predicting Pip's second and final fate, Ishmael suggests that "what
was temporarily subdued in him, in the end was destined to be lu-
ridly illumined by strange wild fires, that fictitiously showed him
off to ten times the natural luster with which in his native Tulland
County in Connecticut, he had once enlivened many a fiddler's
frolic in the green; and at melodious even-tide, with his gay ha-ha!
had turned the round horizon into one star-belled tambourine."

What is Pip's second fate? "I look; you look; he looks; we look; ye
look; they look," he says in "The Doubloon" (C99). This recitation
of the conjugation of the verb "to look" presents a strong contrast
to the idea of seeing—we look, we do not necessarily see. Pip looks

at the doubloon that Ahab has nailed to the mast and sees with his intensified sight that it is "the navel" of the ship. He notes that once nailed to the mast, the doubloon cannot be unscrewed without the ship itself falling apart. So it must stay, eventually to go to the bottom of that ocean where, Ishmael has reported, Pip in his own descent has been granted a wisdom of madness. (The doubloon itself will not be recovered until the day of resurrection.) Pip's madness, in his descent, takes the form of a concentrated focus so intense that he loses a sense of himself; it is a sort of ecstasy. The intense concentration of Pip's madness has everything to do with his repetition of the conjugation of the verb "to look." This repetition of the verb, with its latent imperative form—look, look!—implicitly urges us to think of how we may use words to declare our knowledge of the world while also showing the hopelessness of all our attempts, spoken from a place of madness that Ishmael and Ahab both recognize to contain a reality larger than what we are prepared to accept if we are to remain sane. (The possibility of a healing that is suggested in the dialogue of Pip and Ahab, in which their pairing may serve to repair both, the hope that each could be re-membered by the other, must be refused by Ahab in the name of his obsession with the White Whale, his lost limb, his lost membership in the world of men. Ahab's narrow vision propels him to his tragic fate, whereas Pip's will send him elsewhere.)

Pip's name itself bears yet another clue. His name, as Ishmael notes, is the nickname of Pippin, and one meaning of the word "pip" is seed, so Pip may be thought of as being the seed of an apple, the heart of that which is the original temptation, and the original sin, the knowledge that will drive humanity out of paradise. The OED is instructive on another point as well—Pip is also a shortened version of the word "peep," a word which has among its meanings "to look." Another meaning of pip is the black mark that appears on playing cards and dice, which gives an element of chance to the name itself. Pip's mad looking encompasses all those on board the *Pequod*. He may be thought of as the looker, the peeper, the secret witness to all events, deeply sensitive to the contingency of the event itself. (There are no great expectations for this Pip.)

Pip's madness is not exactly of the same sort as the wisdom of Shakespeare's fool, though like the fool of Lear he imparts wisdom to whoever will listen, especially to Ahab, the king of evil signification. When Ahab sees poor mad Pip berating his absent self, he is touched to the heart, as he is not touched by any other. He makes Pip his constant companion in the captain's cabin until the moment Ahab goes to his final confrontation with the White Whale. Ahab admits that his love of Pip, even after his love of Starbuck, is the last barrier he must surmount to confront the whale. His love of Starbuck is born of one identity—that of the father and husband; his love of Pip is born of another—that of a common abjection. He recognizes how Pip's deep sympathy balances him, distracting him from his monomania, and thus puts at risk his ultimate goal, his confrontation with the White Whale. When Ahab prepares to leave Pip, he explains, "There is that in thee, poor lad, which I feel too curing to my malady. Like cures like, and for this hunt, my malady becomes my most desired health" (C129). Pip protests, urging Ahab to use "poor me for your one lost leg; only tread upon me sir; I ask no more, so I remain a part of ye." Pip's recourse to the first person is a sign of his possible healing, his hope to return to some integration of his self with another. Pip's absence becomes Ahab's presence, the way Ahab is able to begin to gain perspective on his monomania. But because he is more wedded to his whale than to his life, Ahab must leave Pip, leave him alone, more alone than any living soul on the *Pequod*—deserted first by Stubb, and now not only by Ahab, but by himself. Upon Ahab's final departure Pip says, "Here he this instant stood; I stand in his air—but I'm alone. Now were even poor Pip here I could endure it, but he's missing. Pip, Pip!" (C129). Here Pip finally and forever abandons his use of the first person. How more alone can anyone be than to be missing himself as he stands in the air of another? This doubly absent self is yet another clue, for we may ask, who is speaking here? Pip is gone; who speaks in his place?

Charles Olson's discovery that the second draft of *Moby-Dick* was written after Melville read *Lear* enables us to perceive Pip as a truth-telling fool. When Pip loses his mind, he also achieves a strange objectivity, a third-person perspective not uncommon to Shakespeare's fool, a position from which he can comment upon the cruel ironies of the unfolding tragedy. But his comments are less about Ahab, his king, than they are about this other loss of self in the face of the white event. Moreover, Melville provides in Pip what Shakespeare does not provide for his fool—an explanation of the genesis of his madness in abandonment. (In that sense, if Pip indeed be a fool, he may be closer to Tom of Bedlam, the heroic Edgar, than to Lear's constant companion.)

Pip anticipates Ishmael's fate—to float alone, abandoned as thoroughly as Pip himself was. Is Ishmael's entire narrative as mad as Pip's? As wise? Ishmael tells the tale, the lone survivor. We may imagine him as Peretz seems to imagine him, telling this tale in the streets of Martha's Vineyard, wandering the taverns of Manhattan, urgently pressing his narrative upon passersby, chagrined by their indifference, by their glancing recognition that Ishmael may be, like Pip in the end, mad.

Ishmael has a secret. What is it?

Pip and Ishmael, Ishmael and Pip. His fear of being sold turns to terror as Pip floats alone, realizing that Stubb's threat may now be a prophecy of the cabin boy's fate. It is unbearable, this thought. And so Pip ceases to think it. Yet the body of this poor shattered soul remains afloat, adrift, waiting the next turn. What is to become of this unthinking Pip? Is he worthy? That is, does he still possess a worth? For the length of the voyage, as we have seen, Pip's worth is determined by his "lay." How can we not see in this evaluation of worth the core continuity between being bought and being sold?

The Hobbesian formulation of the relationship of worth to price is a root dynamic that is played out fully in *Moby-Dick*. Beyond the hubris of Ahab, underwriting his madness yet apart from it, is the constant calculation of worth that exists in complementary tension with the unfathomable value of the interior life of the lonely self. The attempt to present equivalent values reduces the members of the crew to interchangeable parts of an infernal machine. It also intensifies the relationships that exist among the crew members as they strive to join a common project in order to increase the worth of each and every one, or, put negatively, to escape the harsh valuation of a failed voyage. So, like Pip, Ishmael believes himself to be threatened with the possibility of slavery. Like Pip, Ishmael is a peeper, narrating events that could only be observed from a particular position on the quarterdeck of the *Pequod*. Like Pip, Ishmael is a castaway at sea for a day and night, only fortuitously picked up by the *Rachel* as that ship seeks out its lost crew member. Like Pip, Ishmael is a self at a loss, brilliant and bright, a Connecticut man who has become a New Yorker of the heart no doubt, someone who imagines that upon the sea his lay will not be counted separately from the lay of others.

Let me say it: the tragic engine of *Moby-Dick* is the fact that Ishmael is Pip. The shattered identity of the narrator who demands or suggests or pleads that we call him Ishmael is that which is inhabited by the least significant member of the crew of the *Pequod*, Pip. It is Pip who alone survives to tell the tale, cook's assistant assuming the identity of an imaginary seaman, an insignificant peeper passing with a new identity. It is Pip who is the silent witness to the important and trivial events on board the ship. It is Pip who demands that we call him Ishmael and claims to be a seaman, Pip who imagines himself repelled by the black church he is stumbling into, Pip who claims at first to be repelled by the blackness of his

eventually beloved Queequeg. It is Pip reporting on Pip's descent to
the bottom of the ocean, Pip describing how *he* saw God's foot on
the loom. Pip provides witness to Pip's experience.

All of these incidents in the retelling of the tale assume an ironic,
or perhaps gothic, cast. This *post hoc* identity can easily be understood as simply providing the cook's assistant with a good disguise
as he observes the activities of others, as from his lowly post he
imagines a more elevated station for himself, as he is compelled into
service on Stubb's boat, as his personal experience of the white event
drives him to the dissolution of his very self, and finally as he becomes the closest confidant to the most important personage on
the ship. The dancing, tambourine-playing, bright and brilliant
artist has the sensitivity to describe in detail the ongoing drama of
the *Pequod,* and in being a castaway he anticipates the final fate of
the crew, who will eventually come to see what he has seen, the
deepest depths of the sea.

Who is Pip? Let us imagine him to be as Ishmael suggests, brilliant, but let us imagine something more, perhaps something like
this: the first son of a famous man, a child of the coupling of master
and slave, who takes the name Ishmael because that is who he is—
the lost son, the bastard brother, the founder of the lost tribe (even
if only of the all-one tribe of himself), the neglected, first-born el-
der of the much beloved legitimate son, the black child of Randolph
family miscegenation, he who has another tale to tell of the Patagonian crew of the counter-biblical, demonic, and doomed *Pequod.*

If we imagine Pip to be Ishmael, we may be able to imagine
something more—the urtext of an American self at a loss, shattered
by the tragedy of its own unraveling, unable to cope with the desperate knowledge that every self may be bought or sold, and that
every measure can be reduced to the common denominator of
price. Then the tale yields yet another lesson, for Pip tells us: To be
lonely in America is to be black and brilliant, constantly in danger
of being bought and sold, enmeshed in the deepest genealogy of

power and loss, and a secret witness to a catastrophe that only deepens over time.

The White Event

Peretz suggests that to grasp the fullest meaning of *Moby-Dick* we must understand the fabulous character of the disaster in "the enigmatic realm of the white event of address" (87). Ishmael's encounters with whiteness—of the whale, of Ahab, of the cries and shouts that he voiced and that blended with the voices of the rest of the crew into a white noise—give expression to an irresolvable enigma of identity when confronted with the catastrophe that shatters all possibility of knowing. This catastrophe is nothing less than the experience of the overwhelming sense of life in the face of its destruction, an encounter that demands our complete response. "This wounding call through which the 'me' discovers, ashamed, its living nudity is at the same time a singularizing call and that which dispossesses me, and being exposed to it means that I both have to respond to it, call it by name, and be responsible to it, although I do not know what it wants from me. I also have the task of responding to who I am in front of it, that is, to justify my existence, my life, which is exposed to its judgment" (86). In the end, this responsibility and the impossibility of its resolution are the subject matter of the modern novel. Peretz writes,

> This event's fabulous nature should not be understood as offering some escapist fantasy from reality, for we have seen that the white event as the origin of the fabulous is also a disastrous, traumatic event. The collapse of the "I" involved in this event is a wounding devastation which destroys the "I"'s familiar and stable world. It is thus that the fabulous, the monstrous, and the disastrous open up together and are entangled in the same moment of address, linguistically associated with the cry. (88)

This cry is all that we have in the face of the white event; it is what sets us in motion; it is the heart of the tragedy of modernity itself. This cry, which comes in the form of a call, separates the human from the non-human. It is a howling, the bare minimum below which we cannot fall and still remain human.

It may well be that the collapse of the "I" in the face of the destruction of its world is the signature event of *Moby-Dick*. If that is the case, and if it also is the case that Pip is the narrator of this collapse, then his mysterious survival as Ishmael "to tell the tale" places him in a unique position to comprehend two intertwined political problems—the status of the African-American individual in a culture of enslavement, and the universalizing of the dissolved identity of the castaway as the avatar of lonely being. In this sense, the undoing of the tragedy of African-American experience remains the impossible project of American political thought, and it is the surrogate claim that all Americans must make upon the world, in the end, to save us from ourselves. As we must accept the haunting of chattel slavery, we must move forward to accept that we are haunted as well by the other genocides of identity and power that we have so far refused to confront in our own time. For there is yet another affinity that is called forth by the experience of the lonely self of *Moby-Dick,* the affinity of the ruined and mad chattel slave with the Musselman of the concentration camp, both existing as alternative incarnations of the contemporary form that bare life—what Peretz refers to as "the living nudity"—takes.

This bareness, this exposure to the nothingness of the white event, is the unspoken, perhaps the unspeakable, experience of the lonely self *in extremis.* We are bidden to feel the heart of this darkness, and yet none of us can speak it. The call of the white event plays itself out in the secular history of the Western lands through the active witnessing of a history combined with a subjective stepping outside of it, a participating in the hunt, a wailing as a witness and yet a prophetic imagining of an overcoming of that very history. What Americans have a greater claim to have known the white event than those who experienced the Middle Passage? Torn from their families, transported in shackles to the western shore of Africa, thrown into the black hole of the hold of a slave ship, taken across an unknown ocean to an unknown land, shattered both physically and psychically, singing in the face of an unspeakable and interminable transit, these African immigrants of a different sort came to the eastern shores of the American continent and gave decisive shape to the culture that eventually emerged. They prepared us to know the horror lurking here, the malice at the root. The American sublime, for this is what we may call the experience of the white event, has now come to haunt the entire world—if not in the figures of Vietnamese, Filipinos, Mexicans, Japanese, Amerindians in older adventures of empire, then in the new figures of the abused and humiliated prisoners held in our imperial prison at Abu Ghraib. These events crystallize the enormity of the white event into a single image, make those older claims contemporary, and warn us of the larger catastrophe awaiting the empire we have forgetfully made.

How are we to comprehend Pip's madness in reference to this ongoing catastrophe? Pip floats to the bottom of the existential ocean to witness the expanse of godly wisdom. His descent allows him to see beyond reason, to see behind the mask, "the unwarped primal world." "So man's insanity is heaven's sense; and wondering from all mortal reason; man comes at last to that celestial thought, which to reason, is absurd and frantic; and weal or woe, feels then uncompromised, indifferent as his God" (C93). In his cosmic indifference, Pip is able to witness all, and to speak of God's foot upon the loom. But what does he witness? He dissolves into an observer of himself, perfectly lonely. Ever after, he is a third person. "Where's Pip?" he asks, not knowing this one thing. It is only as Ishmael that he is able to answer the question. This means that he is no longer Pip; that Pip, if present in bodily form, has been absorbed into this new and other identity. This is the schizoid split enacted by the lonely self, the operation that allows you to talk about yourself as though you weren't even there. In this strange sense, Pip becomes a terminus point of the Cartesian self, the ultimate form that the ghostly self takes, no longer knowing who he is.

Pip disappears into this other self who wants to be called Ishmael. He is lost. But what does this mean? Is there a ghostly survival here, a haunting of Ishmael by Pip, and a haunting of all of American literature as a consequence? And if so, how can this literature of the marginal help us in understanding the abject experience of this lonely, insignificant being? If we identify the emergence of Ishmael from the ruins of Pip, we may be able to locate another movement within a larger political narrative, another struggle over the fate of the lonely self at wit's end. To put it in the form of a question, what happens when this most marginal of characters enters the heart of our experience as political subjects?

If Pip represents such a movement out of the total disappearance of a self, Willy Loman's collapse offers no such recourse. He does not replace his self with another self, but kills the self he is, in a false hope for a future. The infernal machine of selling continues along its way, even after death. Ownership is a terminus point of another sort than that of being owned; it offers a sort of weird finality that may be even more difficult to escape. Thoreau once wrote, "It is hard to have a southern overseer; it is worse to have a northern one; and worst of all when you are the slave-driver of yourself."[9] While we may wonder about his clarity concerning better and worse, his point seems straightforward enough: the realization by the self-possessed human that his ownership means he is a slave is a traumatic revelation that he has lost himself. He comes to the knowledge that he is nothing other than another owned being, to be bought and sold.

And yet Willy Loman also struggles toward his own white event, completing his life on terms which may shatter our assumptions about what a good life is, but which nonetheless, in their own way, offer him a movement out of a disaster that is as vast as the world he has experienced. If it is not Willy who will reap the harvest of this event, perhaps it is Biff, the real "nothing man," who goes lower than the low man in order to find another line of flight from the conditions of possessive individualism. Is Biff to Willy as Ishmael is to Pip, the other who is able to articulate most fully the meaning of this loss, this nothingness that informs the pathos of the lonely self?

Pip and Willy are representative men, expressions of the solipsism that is a termination point of the lonely self. Pip is a figment of the imagination of the writer Herman Melville, who would himself die alone, harassed by those to whom he owed money, with no one heeding his urgent and mad stories, his own expressions of the obscure desire to be rid of his lonely self. Pip is no one. Pip is as alone as any figure in the history of literature, the "all-one," the deep thought-diver, call him Ishmael, lost brother, invisible man, split, schizoid, least body on the good ship *Pequod,* eyewitness to the white event, floating in the sea, clinging to the coffin of his one imagined friend, mad, lost, the lonely self. Willy is the creation of that brilliant son of twentieth-century America who recognizes the terrible price of our imperious desire for commodious living. Willy is the low man in the world of number one, where nothing less than number one counts, where the insistence that attention must be paid is ignored, the man from whom we avert our eyes. Arthur Miller succeeds Melville, giving this culture its greatest play as Melville gave us our greatest novel, in pursuit of the same impossible dream.

As we bear witness to these characters, we bear witness to our own ghosts, our own lost and pitiful selves. This is what it means to be lonely in America.

Chapter III

Loving

On the surface of it, the lover wants the beloved. This, of course, is not really the case.

—Anne Carson, *Eros the Bittersweet*

Mother Tongue

Cordelia calculates, divides her love. Paradoxically, she does so in order to provide for her father carefully measured, sincere words of love, all the love a child may give to a father and still remain herself.

But there is more to Cordelia's calculus than finding a way to express love for her father. Cordelia's words are measured in part because she has suffered the loss of her mother. To begin with the problem of the missing mother is, to parody Freud, to begin an analysis that is destined to be interminable. However, this fact does not suggest that we can somehow do otherwise, for the condition of loneliness emerges from our attempts to solve the problem of divided love. This is true not just because Lear's wife was dead at the time of his abdication. There is a broader story of the lonely self in play here, of which the measuring of the love of a daughter for her father is but a part. We humans are torn apart, struggling to return to the source, to the infantine state of a distant re-membering of a primal unity. The complex interplay of language and embodiment inflects our attempts to understand our loneliness. But even the very fact of our language indicates that in the end, as in the beginning, we are of woman born. The matrix shapes the way we express ourselves.

Despite its blatantly sexist overtones, Thoreau's argument in *Walden* regarding language, where he writes about the distinction between mother and father tongues, is pertinent here. "The one is commonly transitory, a sound, a tongue, a dialect merely, almost brutish, and we learn it unconsciously, like the brutes, of our mothers. The other is the maturity and experience of that; if that is our mother tongue, this is our father tongue, a reserved and select expression, too significant to be heard by the ear, which we must be born again in order to speak."[1] The claims that Thoreau makes in this passage are deeply gendered—mother tongue is taught to brutes, father tongue to the brutes upon the achievement of a certain competence—reflecting the division of labor between private and public, home and school. Thoreau emphasizes this difference in order to re-create the experience of birth: out of a mute, brutish beginning, we move forward to the experience of another muteness as the basis for our remembrance of things past. We call it reading and writing, or thinking.

Thoreau's concern is not simply with the import of the father tongue and the claims upon culture that writing might make, but with the silences as well as the sounds that might be heard in such writings, silences and sounds that are otherwise unavailable to our ears. He writes, "What the Roman and Grecian multitude could not *hear,* after the lapse of ages a few scholars *read,* and a few scholars only are still reading it" (354). For Thoreau, this lapse between mother tongue and father tongue points to a hope for a democracy, perhaps a democracy of some indefinite future that is composed of a more general literacy, so that we may all learn to read and hence hear what we otherwise would not be able to hear.

The idea of a *lapse* between the spoken and the read word is of general philosophical importance for Thoreau—his very theory of voice is dependent upon it, because the lapse of time is also for him the primary expression of the general unfolding of a human being.

> No wonder the earth expresses itself outwardly in leaves, it so labors with the idea inwardly. The atoms have already learned this law, they are pregnant by it. The overhanging leaf sees here its prototype. *Internally,* whether in the globe or animal body, it is a moist thick *lobe,* a word especially applicable to the liver and lungs and *leaves* of fat (————, *labor, lapsus,* to flow, or slip downward, a lapsing; ————, *globus,* lobe, globe; also lap, flap, and many other words); *externally,* a dry thin leaf, even as the *f* and *v* are a pressed and dried *b.* The radicals of lobe are *lb,* the soft mass of the *b* (single lobed, or B, double lobed) with the liquid *l* behind it pressing it forward. In globe, *glb,* the guttural *g* adds to the meaning the capacity of the throat . . . The whole tree is but one leaf, and rivers are still vaster leaves whose pulp is intervening earth, and towns and cities are the ova of insects in their axils. (546–547)

In this passage, as in others, Thoreau seems to be trying to have us work the mouth, to have us read aloud the shape of the sounds of the letters that form the words. That the strange specificity of this plunge into the sounds of the words is embedded in a discussion of leaves as a fundamental structure of life is not an accident. Thoreau hopes to remind us of the deepest connections of words to embodiment, and embodiment to the world. The guttural *g* employs the throat, which amplifies the mouth's self-awareness of the sonority

of speech and its preservation in the letters of the words that connect the written back to the spoken. Thoreau seems to be both
highlighting the distance between written and spoken word, and
showing us a way to recompose ourselves through a bodily reenact-
ment of the primal moment of their separation. The lips to which
he refers are not only those of the mouth but of the labia, and the
labor of birthing a child is metaphorically akin to the labor of birthing a word. This connection of the visual to sonority through the
guttural mouthing of the letters of the word leads us to reflect upon
the continuities underlying the separate moments of the two
mouths—shaping words at one point, opening us to the world at
another—as organs of birthing. This moment of reconciliation of
mother and father may be thought of as Thoreau's sense of voice. I
imagine it would also serve as an alternative to Lear's response to
the measured words of Cordelia.

This sense of voice is a part of Thoreau's deeper understanding of
and commitment to embodiment. He imagines a birthing of the
human that is both deeply embedded in the claims of our experience or mother tongue and yet otherworldly, a fatherly birthing,
beyond the possibilities of the currently human even as it resides so
deeply within the biblical allegory of the shaping of Adam from a
ball of clay.

> What is man but a mass of thawing clay? The ball of the human
> finger is but a drop congealed. The fingers and toes flow to their
> extent from the thawing mass of the body. Who knows what
> the human body would expand and flow out to under a more
> genial heaven? Is not the hand a spreading *palm* leaf with its
> lobes and veins? The ear may be regarded, fancifully, as a lichen,
> *umbilicaria*, on the side of the head, with its lobe or drop. The
> lip—*labium*, from *labor*(?)—laps or lapses from the sides of the
> cavernous mouth. (547–548)

This lapsing of the lips, or labor of the mouth, is the way Thoreau connects the reading and speaking of a new language to the event of rebirth. It is a labor of the lips that occurs when we adopt the father tongue, when the language we read becomes the language we speak through the lapse between the written and the spoken word. This is an employment of voice that returns words to speech, to the body, as a way of converting us to new meanings.

Is this not also the scandal of language, the implied abandonment of the mother every time we write? Is this the scandal that must remain unspoken in *Lear,* that we are moved away from the mother as the non-negotiable term for the acceptance of our inheritance? How can we demand reconciliation or peace with the missing mother when we repudiate her every time we speak? Perhaps it is better to remain silent, but then again, perhaps not.

Scene One: The War at Home

In the life of my marriage, the moment arrived when it became impossible to reconcile the idea of togetherness within the household with the idea of holding a place in the world. My wife and I fought over time, and that fight, extending over several years, was the worst we ever experienced together. I suspect this passage occurs in many marriages, and that the tensions become most acute when the partners overtly agree to share an equal burden in running the household, especially in marriages that issue in children, and covertly continue to inhabit their old assumptions about the value of their own time versus that of their partner. The claustrophobia of constancy, the irritation that builds as passion turns into habit, as wonder at the infancy of new children becomes the toil of caretaking, as the challenges and excitement of work and social life infringe upon the grind of home economics, when week by week one member of the couple is doing more to sustain the home than the other—these conditions of our life together hit both of us very hard. Sometimes marriage, the simple idea of a joining in love, seemed absurd to us. What we had instead was a quiet war. Brenda would use that metaphor explicitly, referring to our situation as a tug-of-war, an ugly game where one of us would pull toward our own work and outside life and the other would fall into the mud-pit of diapers and laundry and working and shopping. Again and again we would negotiate cease-fires, sometimes long-term truces, but eventually one of us would violate the terms and off we would go again. We tried to balance our outside demands and desires for recognition with our responsibilities to each other, and eventually we were exhausted by the effort.

But as we were being worn down, something else was occurring. The two creatures we held responsible for our diminished circumstances, our loss of freedom and descent into the mind-numbing work of sustaining their existence, were becoming human beings. Our children, great distractions that they were from our so-called lives, asserted themselves as integral parts of the very real lives we were coming to lead. Not because they were exceptional—of course they were and are, as are all children in our bucolic New England college town—but because their trajectory through childhood provided us with a measure of our own passage into adulthood. Instead of the constant repetition of the diurnal turns of habit, they called forth from us another response. This does not mean that the normalcy of family life was something we embraced, or that we thought our childless friends somehow were "missing" something essential to their development as adults. On the contrary, it was simply how we ourselves were becoming adults. Our path was different from that of my parents (or for that matter, that of Willy and Linda Loman); it was determined not by the struggle of one person to come to some form of success, and the dependence of the family on him, but by a more open and explicitly negotiated sense of what a family ought to be.

It was shocking for me to learn that others sometimes thought of me as being a good parent, convinced as I had always been that I was not competent at anything other than reading, writing, and (maybe) teaching, realizing as I did how badly I had been raised, and realizing as well how difficult it is to break with that past in raising my own kids, especially trying to overcome the intergenerational transmission of anger (sometimes secretly accusing my toddler daughter of ruining my life, for instance; sometimes imagining throwing my infant son against the wall of his bedroom if he didn't stop his crying, shut his eyes, and finally allow me to leave his nursery). But the way I was raised, I also found, was a part of what I always will be—puzzled, wondering, trying to figure out how I came to be who I am. In this sense, I found that thinking about the conditions of the family and its place in a larger context in itself doesn't really hurt in the raising of children—that the overt quality of the struggle Brenda and I had with each other, including both the anger and the humor, was somehow an avoidance of the avoidance of love, a stumble-step forward in a culture still dominated by the separating powers of possession and dispossession. We talked to each other, and the conversation became an endless reevaluation of our values, conducted with the wit and care (and the mutual hurting that only true intimates can impose on each other) that came to define the shape of our comfort with each other, despite other shortcomings.

I try not to imagine what my children were thinking as their parents struggled to cope with the fact of their place in our lives, nor do I attempt to imagine what they may be thinking now. The distance between my memory of my own childhood and the present reality of their lives yawns wide enough so that when I refer back to my own memories, the past, alive as it is for me, is simply not comparable to their present. But do I remember with accuracy the feelings of my own childhood? The gap between that past and the present seems to me to be unbridgeable, but this is also the gap we constantly try to close, the persistent space between the parallel lines of these memories. When my children remember their childhood, perhaps they will know better than I the sources of their heartbreak and joy.

For me the fact that we will fail to reconcile past to present is less important than *how* we will fail to do so. It is something never to be accomplished, this idea of a reconciliation with one's past. It will always be an unquiet memory. For the comedy and tragedy that go back to the beginning of familial experience are both intertwined with that gap—tragedy with the failure to negotiate our way to reconciling ourselves to its persistence, as in the sad tale of Lear, and comedy in our successful surrender to its continued presence in our lives.

One way we persist in trying to bridge this unbridgeable gap is by pretending that we can actually know our children. We observe our children, and in observing them imagine that we have somehow shaped them. I especially think of the moment recalled by most parents in our culture—not the moment of birth itself, but the morning when the new baby is brought home from the hospital, and there you are, totally responsible for this incredibly frail and inarticulate yet unbelievably demanding thing. Every moment now becomes a measure of progress toward their autonomy, toward the moment when our minors become majors and we can once again imagine ourselves as autonomous adults—but now with other adults whom we have created, surrounding us with pure love and perfect peace. And then we can imagine being alone, remarrying, perhaps even remarrying that person to whom we have been married all along. It is as if life has a map for us, as if we are following a plan that we can control, as if we can, by being the best parents we know how to be, get to a happy ending. As if.

These are not new insights, of course. John Locke wrote with clarity and startling straightforwardness about parental authority over children in the late seventeenth century:

> Their parents have a sort of rule and jurisdiction over them,
> when they come into the world, and for some time after; but it
> is a temporary one. The bonds of this subjection are like the
> swaddling clothes they art wrapt up in, and supported by, in the
> weakness of their infancy: age and reason, as they grow up,
> loosen them, till at length they drop quite off, and leave a man
> at his own free disposal.[2]

Locke was concerned about parental authority and its limits because he wished to distinguish between political power justly derived from reason and political power derived from a misconstrued
paternal authority that falsely justifies sovereign absolutism. The
swaddling clothes of subjection were designed to give way to, or
even somehow produce, the internal bonds of reason and maturity.
When we reach the age of reason, we are prepared to assume the
role of citizen. Over time we parents watch our children grow, first
steps leading to second steps, first words leading to sentences, the
passionate unreason of adolescence leading to the calm adults before us, who are now strangers to us, beings who are now free. This
is supposed to be the heart of the matter for families, and it is its
own argument for the persistence of the family in whatever form it
takes.

The Lockean vision of the growth of children into the freedom
of reason has had a multitude of critics over the centuries. Reason
often appears as a form of imprisoning power, and swaddling clothes
can easily turn into the chains of a slave. We know that the picture
of the family as a gentle shaper of the children of the household is
incomplete at best—that Oedipal rage, the cold assessment of a
specifically paternal power and the repression of maternal care, the
obsessions of erotic love, equally well fit the picture of the family.
Alternatively, the rage of the mother, the repression of the child
out of a misplaced desire for control of what is in the end uncon-
trollable, also leads to familial disaster. Practical power overwhelms

us, leads us into temptation, ironically prevents us from being reasonable.

Moreover, the power of reason is too easily contrasted with the powers of unreason, so that the specific customs through which people come into their own as subjects are assumed too quickly to be coterminous with subjectivity itself. We embrace identities of convenience—husband, wife, son, daughter. But in our time many of us have been asking questions about what counts as an identity. For instance, what do we make of the family composed of Heather and her two mommies? Assuming that we are the ones who wrap our children in swaddling clothes, can we so wrap them as to encourage them to grow up gay? What of the family composed only of adults, bound together by elective affinities, mutual attractions? Can we regard that family as a family at all? What of the polygamous family, bound together through a perceived injunction from God in which the submission of the wives to the authority of the father is seen as the sign of a great blessing?

These questions point to the variety of familial experience, especially when we imagine the family along the dimensions outlined by Locke and his many successors. And yet we are also confined in our thinking about families by our own memories. These memories matter, even if they are not explicitly invoked in order to justify the present or future. Is it possible to capture a sense of the lonely isolation of childhood moments, the framing of memory that would enable us to prepare for the future? Should we know enough to open up the Freudian machine and make peace with the ghosts of our past selves? Or should we be condemned to a violent repetition of this melancholic scene?[3]

These are familiar questions, however oddly I have posed them here. But the form of questioning is only designed to highlight the stakes that we have claimed about the power of family life to shape who we are. Nonetheless, we also know that civilization is a precarious venture. We are always on the verge of decadence, moral failure, the terrible sacrifice of all that we have worked for to build a civilization of power and propriety. Because we want what is best for our children, we will do anything we can to ensure that their lives will be good ones. But what if this desire is a part of the loneliness we feel? As we sacrifice for our children, it may be that we will learn that no sacrifice is great enough. As we work, we may learn that there is no assurance that our work will not be in vain. And as we learn to forgo the pleasures of the bittersweet, it may be that only then will we learn most completely the lessons of regret.

In all of these struggles we may come to realize that we are grasping for something across a boundary—that of the memory of desire—that is not to be crossed without the sacrifice of some of our most cherished illusions concerning our connection to the world. There are powerful forces at work on both sides of that boundary. Any time that we seek to gain access to the dreamscape of childhood, we must remain suspicious of our motives. Upon achieving our majority status, we may pretend to return to our prior status as minors, but this pretense is of no help in the end, for we remain in the sway of our adult selves. So this is a border crossing fraught with danger.

And it is not only our illusion that we can restore an innocence to our desire that makes it dangerous to return to childhood. There is a monster on the other side of that boundary: our own former selves. It may be that our concern to protect our children is also a concern to protect our selves from the truth about our own innocence and its lack. In our culture, because we are so good at expressing our anxiety concerning the need to protect our children from the ravages of adult predators, we fail to confront a deeper fear concerning our guilt about the desires of our earlier self. Nonetheless, if we are to reach some sense of understanding of our selves, we are almost duty-bound to cross the boundaries between majority and minority that we have so carefully tried to maintain. We must do so, not simply in pursuit of happiness, but in recognition that in that pursuit lies a key toward a better caring for those we love. In fact, the shape of our desire to protect our children is often a means by which we avoid that deeper confrontation and that deeper level of care. It's still the same old story—the more we desire to do the right thing, the more likely we are to fail. How could this be so?

This drama is underwritten by what Foucault called the perverse implantation of the family, which he saw as being at the core of the modern history of sexuality. Writing of the nineteenth-century family, a family that persists into the present, he understood it not only as a scene of monogamy, that is, as the establishment of the nuclear family that so firmly inhabits our imagination as the model for the family, but as the core of a more complex network.

> [The family] was also a network of pleasures and powers linked together at multiple points and according to transformable relationships. The separation of grown-ups and children, the polarity established between the parents' bedroom and that of the children . . ., the relative segregation of boys and girls, the strict instructions as to the care of nursing infants . . ., the attention focused on infantile sexuality, the supposed dangers of masturbation, the importance attached to puberty, the methods of surveillance suggested to parents, the exhortations, secrets, and fears, the presence—both valued and feared—of servants: all this made the family, even when brought down to its smallest dimensions, a complicated network, saturated with multiple, fragmentary, and mobile sexualities.[4]

This family, the lonely family, is torn open by the stresses of its desires, but also by the demands that it cohere, that it hold itself together against the very forces that it incites into existence. If we explore some of the narratives of family loneliness that reflect this tension, we may go some way toward understanding this dilemma, which is a dilemma of love. As full as our hearts may become in the presence of those whom we love, as empty as they will be upon our abandonment, it is in the family that the threads of lonely love are woven together, and unravel as well.

Absent Presence

A man is walking across a barren desert landscape, following the straight line of a path known only to himself. He carries an empty plastic jug. He comes to a settlement on the side of a road, where there is a cantina. After testing a water faucet outside that has no water, he walks inside to the cool darkness, reaches for some ice in a bin, starts to eat the ice, and collapses onto the floor. This man, named Travis, is returning from nowhere, reentering life after a two-year period in which he had disappeared from the world of those who knew him. He is silent, traumatized by some terrible event. He carries a card with a name and phone number on it. The doctor who examines him calls the number and reaches Travis's brother Walt in Los Angeles. Once informed of Travis's reappearance and physical condition, Walt travels to a border town in Texas to get him, with the goal of bringing him to Walt's home in California. Walt has news for Travis—he and his wife Ann have been taking care of Travis's son Hunter, who arrived on their doorstep with a note shortly after Travis disappeared four years ago. Apparently Hunter had been left there by Travis's wife, Jane, before she too disappeared.

This is the first act in a creative collaboration between the German director Wim Wenders and the American playwright Sam Shepard, a movie called *Paris, Texas*.[5] Released in 1984, it won the Grand Prize, the Palme d'Or, at the Cannes Film Festival, and while it created a bit of a stir upon its release in the United States, it soon faded from view and became a cult film, especially admired by fans of Wenders as one of his true masterpieces. Among its other themes, the film is a sustained meditation on the fate of the American West.

And as the West itself comes to be a metaphor for the possibilities of our future, the very spaciousness of the film encourages us to think about the meaning of emptiness and the habitations of the human. Travis is a liminal man. He walks a line that follows the arc of electrical power strung across desolate spaces; he is out of place wherever he is. His fate, though, always remains tied to that of his family, however far he may have retreated into the emptiness of himself. The theme of the film is how the lonely family comes together and falls apart in the landscape of the West. It is in the end a love story, but of a very particular kind, one that refuses to allow us to seek redemption in our selves.

In his commentary on the DVD of the film, Wenders explains that he and Shepard began with a simple vision of a person who comes out of nowhere and seems to be going nowhere. Hence they immediately take on the themes that inform the lonely self—when we come to the place that is nowhere, we are confronting our skepticism at its deepest level. To return from nowhere is to confront that skepticism, to begin to live through it, to make a step toward a recovery or re-membering of oneself. The rubble of this western land evokes the end of a dream of the future, with no restoration of the ruins of a past. (The first part of the film was shot in sequence, and the opening scene is set in the barren landscape of Big Bend, Texas, in the southwest corner of the state. But it is not pristine; there is litter, rusty machinery, the rubble of cast-off parts that is often found on the edge of rural settlements. Wenders never tries to hide the detritus of the human as it pollutes that landscape.) Travis's simple act of walking—a parody and/or imitation of Thoreau's idea of what walking ought to be—continually demonstrates this precarious relationship of past to future.

In an early scene, after Walt has located his brother and checked both of them into a motel so he can shop for clothes and shoes to replace Travis's rags, Travis takes off again, after seeing himself in a mirror (which appears to cause him excruciating pain and shame).

This time he follows a railroad track. When Walt catches up to him, he asks, "You mind telling me where you're headed, Travis? What's out there? There's nothing out there." That there is nothing out there is the point: it is where Travis wishes to return after having seen his own face. Why?

The answer to this question unfolds slowly, in a rhythm that is almost totally at odds with the conventions of contemporary commercial films. This is a film of conversations, painful, difficult conversations, often composed of silences, conversations that unfold against natural backdrops that seem to be artificial but that are as close to real as can be represented, painstakingly captured by the director and cinematographer. (Michael Shapiro has remarked of the backdrop, filled as it is with signs and words, that it fulfills Wenders's ambitions to read the landscape of the West as fragmented and disordered.) The landscape of the film participates in the conversation—the town of Terlingua (literally, "third language") gestures toward the international feeling of the film, as well as the languages spoken by the different members of Hunter's extended family: Spanish, French, American English. The emptiness of the landscape, even in the city scenes in which the silences deepen, help to cast these conversations as momentous interventions. In each scene, placed against a backdrop of a landscape or in a car, something of import is said, even if it is in language that at first glance seems banal.

For instance, the first words that Travis speaks in the film, after his long silence, come during the long car trip back to Los Angeles. Walt, exasperated, demands that Travis speak, and then threatens to be silent himself. "Damn it I'm your brother, man. You can talk to me. I'm tired of doing all the talking." This first prodding produces nothing, but the next day Walt gets a response to his complaint/ threat when he says: "I'm getting a little sick of the silent routine. You can talk. I can be silent too, you know." This is the moment when Travis finally speaks. He responds to Walt by saying, "Paris,

Paris, Paris." And it turns out that the idea of Paris will be the touchstone for his recovery.

It is worth noting that Walt's demand of Travis to speak is an eerie echo of Lear's demand that Cordelia speak again. But Walt's demand is filial, not paternal; indeed he is tired of the paternal burden of speech, he is weary of his responsibility to be the one who cares, the one who must support a brother who will eventually take the son that he loves away from him. Travis is a cipher to him, and his silence only intensifies the mystery of his return. Walt's demand and Travis's response thus set in motion the wheels, not of tragedy, but of a strange recovery from the consequences of the tragic in everyday life.

Eventually, in fragments and hesitant starts, it is revealed that the Paris on Travis's mind is not Paris, France, but Paris, Texas. In his commentary on the film, Wenders notes that these two words capture the heart of the weird paradox that is Travis's life. A tiny town in the middle of rural Texas is named after the great French capital, or, as Walter Benjamin once put it, the capital of the nineteenth century. Travis later explains that this town was the place and time of his conception, if not of his birth—his very real beginning. He shows Walt a picture of a vacant lot, a photo of dirt and rocks, and explains that he owns it, that it is a lot in Paris, Texas. Walt notes, "There's nothing on it." He asks why Travis bought it, and Travis says that he has forgotten. For Travis, origin conjoins with forgetting, and forgetting links to remembering—it is immediately after this exchange that Travis asks Walt what their mother's "very first name" was, by which he means her maiden name. In this drama there is no mother and no father either, even as it is replete with mothers and fathers. The achievement of parenthood out of the isolation of love may be thought of as one of its themes.

Travis is the nowhere man, trying to remember a lost origin, coming into language again to recover from a loss so great that it made him forget himself. He is also out of time, in the sense that he seems to believe that there is a timelessness to his existence, and yet he recognizes that he must return to a world where time has passed, even as he has failed to mark this time. As they are driving back to California—Travis refuses to fly, refuses to leave the ground—in conversation over dinner in a diner, Walt comments, "You've been gone a long time." Travis replies by asking, "Is four years a long time?" And Walt answers, somewhat urgently, "It is for a boy. It's half his life."

Lost time weighs upon these men, and it is brought into focus through the son they now have in common, Hunter. As a result of the disappearance and then reappearance of Travis, Hunter has two families: his dad Walt and his mom Ann, and his dad Travis and his mom Jane. Hunter will go on a search for his mom Jane, leaving Ann in California and driving to Houston with his dad Travis. This family will reunite, but in the end the family will not be together. Travis will disappear again as Jane and Hunter come together.

This is a film of conversations, punctuated by two remarkable monologues. The family drama has its climax in a conversation between Travis and Jane, which culminates in a long monologue by Travis through which he tells a story, and during which the core secret of the family tragedy is revealed. His final meetings with Jane occur in her place of employment, a peepshow called "The Keyhole Club" in a seedy neighborhood on the outskirts of downtown Houston. The booth is set up in a way that keeps Jane from seeing Travis; he speaks to her through a telephone as she looks into a one-way mirrored window. The camera work in these scenes is amazing—the viewer sees reflection upon reflection, a face looking for and not seeing the other, the other face in hiding, but seeing all. But the cinematography in this film is always in the service of the characters and their story, only telling what is to be told, and no more.

Travis's only hope is to return Hunter to Jane. After seeing Jane for the first time in Houston, prior to the meeting when he reveals

himself to her, he realizes that the pain of their common past cannot be overcome. As he puts it in a recording to Hunter—his good-
bye to him as he leaves him in a hotel room—"The biggest thing
I'd hoped for can't come true. I know that now. You belong together
with your mother." But not with him. Something happened. "It
left me alone in a way I haven't gotten over." His aloneness is to be
his final resting place, but not before he sees Jane one last time. He
needs to repair something, even if he himself is not to be repaired.

In his final meeting with Jane, Travis tells the story of their love
and his marriage to her, but he does so in the third person. "Can I
tell you something?" he asks, sitting in the peepshow booth, on the
other side of the glass from her. She sits down to listen, at first not
knowing who he is. He turns his back on her, focuses on the telephone. It is a simple story, almost archetypal in its description of
the context within which domestic violence erupts.

> *Two people. They were in love with each other. Girl young, beauti-*
> *ful, 17 or 18 I guess; guy quite a bit older, raggedy, wild. Together*
> *they turned everything into a kind of adventure. She liked that.*
> *Going to the grocery store was an adventure. Always together. Very*
> *happy. He loved her. So he quit work, just to be home with her.*
> *Soon she started to worry . . . about money. He got torn inside. He*
> *needed to work, but he couldn't stand to be away from her. He*
> *started imagining things. He'd accuse her of being with other men*
> *in the trailer. Yes. They lived in a trailer home.* (At this point,
> Jane's facial expressions show that she is aware that it is Travis
> on the other side of the glass.) *He started to drink, real bad, and*
> *stayed out late to test her. See if she'd get jealous. But she didn't. He*
> *thought if she didn't get jealous she didn't love him. Then she told*
> *him she was pregnant . . . She started to change. She got irritated*
> *about everything around her. For two years he struggled to pull*
> *them together again . . . He hit the bottle again. This time he got*
> *mean. She dreamed about escaping. He tied a cowbell to her ankle.*

*Tied her to the stove. Laid there listening to her scream and to his
son scream. For the first time he wished he were far away, somewhere without language or streets. When he woke up he was on fire.
Then he ran, he never looked back at the fire. He ran until every
sign of man had disappeared.*

We have heard this story before, it is the common script of familial violence: the man who fuses love to possession, who is "torn inside" by his overwhelming desire to be with his beloved, whose way
of being with her is to control her totally. He tests her by trying to
make her jealous, but he is only projecting his own insecurity on
her, and so he feels worse when she doesn't become like him. Jealousy is the emotion of possession at risk. Yet the more one tries to
possess absolutely, the more resistance to possession one finds. In
this monologue the compression of language, the compression of
time, the dreamlike quality of the scene as Travis describes it, speaking the story—made more compelling by the power of the voice
and haunted eyes of Harry Dean Stanton than it would have been
with a flashback to the flat brutality of a bullying father and husband striking out against those whom he loves—gets to an elemental truth concerning the paradoxical impossibility of love.

Travis's hope is to be somewhere without language or streets.
This is a wish to disappear from the human, to move away from all
signs of civilization, to reject both mother and father tongue. It is a
dream of total privatization, of the privation of the human in the
hope of some relief from the pain of love. This is an impossible
hope, but it is nonetheless where his love has led him, to a loneliness so profound as to make him disappear from himself.

In her meditation on Eros, Anne Carson explains the impossible
logic of what she calls the edge:

> Eros is an issue of boundaries. He exists because certain bound-
> aries do. In the interval between reach and grasp, between "I

love you" and "I love you, too," the absent presence of desire comes alive. But the boundaries of time and glance and I love you are only aftershocks of the main, inevitable Boundary that creates Eros: the boundary of flesh and self between you and me. And it is only, suddenly, at the moment when I would dissolve that boundary, I realize I never can.[6]

Carson observes how the "absent presence of desire," rather than localizing the more general dilemma of being present to the problem of erotic love, indicates the opposite, how erotic love *is* the general dilemma with which we are presented. In the film this erotic tension is played out as an incestuous love embrace in the mother-and-child reunion of Jane and Hunter, with Hunter wrapping his legs completely around Jane's middle, each of them looking deeply into the other's eyes.

But more immediately, when Travis flees from the burning bed he is propelled through his own corporeality into the possibility of psychic dissolution. It is a path he must travel alone, and it is only in the opening shot of the film that we get a glimpse of the desolation of his experience. Traversing the boundary again, echoing geographically the trauma of absent presence along the Texas/Mexican border, Travis is gone for four years—disappeared, thought dead by the rest of the world. His return is shocking, because the boundary he crossed should have killed him. But somehow, implausibly, he has survived.

And yet while he is gone he is not forgotten, even though a certain forgetfulness may have been what Walt and Ann would have wished for in retrospect. Their heartbreak as the stepmother and stepfather who give up their child to a father who has demonstrated in the past and will continue to demonstrate his inability to attend to the needs of his son would be almost unbelievable, if in fact they had given him up to that father. Ann, who by telling Travis of her contact with Jane sets in motion the journey from Los Angeles back

to Houston, is always suspicious of Travis's motives, even as she
clearly is sympathetic to his heartbreak, enough so that she reveals
the confidential information concerning Jane (information she
doesn't even share with her husband, Walt). These Lockean parents
deserve better, and surely Travis deserves worse, in reference to
Hunter. But Travis is seeking to reestablish a boundary, and his act
is to give the son back to the mother.

Travis takes Hunter with him, a surprise that is no surprise. The
agency of this child in the end propels all of these characters into
the future. Hunter, with his Star Wars sheets on his bed and his familiarity with flying through space—in a key conversation with
Travis as they are on the road, he shows a garbled familiarity with
the paradoxes of the speed of light and time travel—demonstrates
his worthiness to go to Houston, the city that controls the space
missions of the United States (yet another paradoxical place). In
fact, it is Hunter who insists that he is to come with Travis. "I want
to come with. I want to find her, too," he says, when he learns of
Travis's plan. Whereas Travis will never fly—he explains to Walt at
one point that "I'm not afraid of heights, I'm afraid of falling"—
Hunter is preparing to go into outer space. He is a child of the future, and his father appears as the unwelcome presence of the past.
This contrast is most clearly presented in an early exchange between
Hunter and Walt, after Hunter has refused to walk home from
school with Travis. Trying to change the subject from his shunning
of Travis, Hunter asks Walt a question: "When are they going to
make space ships like they make cars?" Walt insists, "Travis went to
meet you at school and he wanted to walk you home." Hunter responds, "Nobody walks."

Travis walks. He is defined by walking. He is no flaneur; he walks
to erase boundaries, following electric lines, railroad tracks. He is
nobody, nobody who walks. (His refusal to fly home to Los Angeles
with Walt, resulting in their long drive across the southwestern
landscape, is a consequence not only of his fear of falling, but of his

fear of losing touch with the land itself.) Hunter recognizes his father as nobody, and it will be Travis's challenge to become somebody if he is to be a suitable traveler for his son. He needs to move
from being nobody to becoming Hunter's father. His first step in
this direction, to be able to claim that he has the right to take
Hunter away, is to change his dress from the working-man clothes
that Walt bought for him in Texas to some of Walt's finer clothing,
a three-piece suit, symbolically supplanting Walt's authority in his
own home and assuming his proper position as the older brother.
Aided by the Mexican housekeeper, Aver, who finds the suit and
tells him, "To be a rich father, Senor Travis, you must look to the
sky and never to the ground!" he tries to explain that he is looking
to look like a father, to which she gives the rejoinder that there are
only rich fathers and poor fathers, no in-between. So Travis assumes
the dress of the rich father, looks to the sky, and becomes a patri-
arch to his son. His diminished estate does not matter. And while
the suit is a bit cheesy, probably on its way to be recycled, costume-
like and completed with an overdone fedora, this costume-like
quality of his new outfit emphasizes the fact that it is a role that
Travis is assuming, not a right he is reclaiming. Nonetheless he is as
much a sovereign as Lear at this moment, putting on the robes of
power, even though his renunciation of his kingdom will carry different consequences than for Lear.

By putting on the suit of the rich father and showing up at school
to take Travis back to Walt and Ann's house, Travis becomes real as
a father to Hunter. Hunter explains to his friend who had given
him a ride home on the previous day, so he could avoid walking
with Travis, that the man waiting to walk him home on this day is
his father. His friend is surprised, knowing that Walt is Hunter's
dad. So he asks, "How could you have two fathers?" Hunter replies,
"Just lucky, I guess." Hunter has two fathers, and he also has two
mothers. This doubling of parents, while seen by Hunter as pleni-
tude, compounds the complicated kinships and renunciations at

play in this film—an interweaving of brothers and wives, of disappointments and hopes, all centered on the future of this child. It is as though, instead of filial piety being expected of the child in exchange for an estate, the parents are to be renewed in their lives to the extent that they are able to find a way to articulate their love for the child. But it is always a love that will be expressed eccentrically, off center, through abandonment as well as embrace.

Ann, Walt's wife and stepmother to Hunter, would seem to be the exception; because she has been so close to him, she is the one who has benefited the most from the presence of Hunter in her life and stands to lose the most when he leaves. Ann indicates that she knows she will lose Hunter from the moment she learns from Walt of the reappearance of Travis. She nonetheless provides Travis with the information concerning Jane's location, information that results in Travis's leaving for Houston and taking Hunter with him. Why does she do this? Her admission to Travis comes immediately after she has had an argument with Walt concerning Travis and Hunter. Walt insists that Travis must be helped, even if it means that Hunter goes with him, because, after all, Travis is Hunter's father. Ann realizes how fragile her hold is—she wants to help Travis, but she also wants to keep Hunter. When Hunter calls home to let Ann and Walt know that he has gone with Travis, Ann lies down on Hunter's bed, which is covered with the Star Wars sheets, and weeps. Immediately afterward, we see Hunter in bed at the motel, as he says to Travis, "I'm so used to calling her 'Mom.'"

This is the last reference to Ann in the film. The missing mother in this story, Jane, is to be recovered, as Ann, the Lockean parent, is lost. A substitution occurs. Something is given up so that something can be recovered. What?

Jane, the missing mother, is represented as a cipher of Travis's dispossession until the very end, when her agency as an abused woman who overcomes abuse, however violently, is revealed as the key act of the film. In her barely veiled erotic reunion with Hunter, she is finally fulfilled as a mother. In the plot of the film Jane appears first in the film within the film, the home movie that is shown to Travis at Walt's home in California. Walt insists on showing the movie, seemingly to get Travis to begin to talk to him about what had happened to bring Travis to his current condition. Everyone who is watching this home movie is in it—Walt, Ann, Travis, Hunter. Jane is in the movie too, and thus her absence is made palpable. It is a heartbreaking home movie, revealing a simple love, a united family vacationing on the Texas gulf coast, playful, mugging for the camera as a Mexican accordion melody plays on the soundtrack. No words are spoken, either in the movie, which is silent, or in the living room, which is quiet. But from that moment on, we know that a journey to Jane is how this story will find its resolution.

For all the complexities of this film, there remains a simplicity. The deepest desires we possess are for the things that constantly recede from us. Travis's archetypal response to the demands of desire—jealousy—deepens to the point where he wants to obliterate all lines between him and his beloved, so extending the moment of desire that he may pretend that the boundary between himself and Jane will never be reestablished. But Jane realizes that for him to win, she must lose, completely. The unexpected but inevitable act in this drama is Jane's rebellion—setting fire to their home, burning the marital bed. But this is also the act that forces her to give up her son to the care of her husband's brother. Her autonomy is bought at the price of the loss of her child.

Jane's job in Houston as a stripper in a peepshow reestablishes some of the lines and boundaries. The complex reflections in the mirrored window, the mediated telephonic communications from the client to Jane's room, her ability to speak as well as listen over the phone, all serve to establish a paradoxical barrier, both visual and symbolic, that puts her at a distance from the ordinary claims of sexual desire. Jane's distance could be interpreted as trauma or as power. In the wake of her violent act, it may be both. But the erotic character of her job also anticipates her motherly/erotic embrace of Hunter at the end of the film.

So Jane's action frees them all, though it is a harsh freedom they find, the freedom of emptiness. This is the most profoundly hollow negative freedom that was once famously placed at the core of liberalism by Isaiah Berlin—a freedom of negation, of unimpeded flow, of loss, of lack, of nothingness. In this drawdown to nothingness in the film, a residue of the sovereignty of Lear shows itself again. The members of this lost family become the successors of Lear and his children, only this time it is a Lear with a worthy queen and a son who knows that he is going to propel himself into space, completing the cycle of love and loss as the lonely self finds itself once again at the end of the road, looking forward to a new world. Nothing comes of nothing. But there is another turn to be made.

Navigation to Nowhere

I mentioned earlier that there are two monologues that punctuate this film. Travis's tale of renunciation and repair near the conclusion generates a hope for the future. But there is an earlier moment in the film that is disturbing, and casts doubt against the possibility of any such hope. This scene occurs after Ann has told Travis that she knows of Jane's location in Houston, and Travis is on his way to tell Walt that he plans to go find her. He is walking again, early in the morning, in a predawn landscape of backstreet Los Angeles. He passes a bodega and moves onto a bridge that crosses over a major southern California freeway, eight lanes in each direction (probably the San Diego freeway, north of Los Angeles, leading into the San Fernando valley). As he walks along, he begins to hear the voice of a man who is screaming at the top of his lungs. His words are initially unclear, distant, lost in the hum of the cars below. As Travis walks closer, the words become clearer. As he comes in sight of the man, he stops and listens to him. The screaming man issues a prophecy:

> *You will all be caught with your diapers down! That is a promise! I make you this promise on my mother's head! For right here, today, standing on the very head of my mother, which is our God Green Earth, which everybody who wasn't born in a fucking sewer ought to know and understand to the very marrow of their bones! They will invade you in your beds! They will snatch you from your hot tubs! They will pluck you right out of your fancy sports cars! There is nowhere! Absolutely nowhere in this Godforsaken valley! I'm talking about from the range of my voice right here, clear out to the goddamn Mojave Desert and beyond that! Clear out past Barstow and everywhere else in the valley all the way to Arizona! None of that area will be called a Safety Zone! There will be no Safety Zone! I can guarantee you the Safety Zone will be eliminated! Eradicated! You will all be extradited to the Land of No Return! It's a Navigation to Nowhere! And if you think that's going to be fun, you've got another think coming! I may be a slime-bucket but believe me, I know what the hell I'm talking about! I'm not crazy! And don't say I didn't warn you! I warned you! I warned all of you!*

The prophecy of the screaming man is both specific to the California we know as a place of the postmodern fantastic—a desert megalopolis incapable of sustaining itself—and generalized to humanity—the law of extradition covers everyone, we all have it coming, this trip on the road to nowhere. The screaming man begins with a reminder of our infantine state—diapers down, born of mother, snatched from our playthings, taken from our warm and snuggly beds, naked in our tubs, we will suffer a great loss. What is that loss? The film was made in the early 1980s, a period of the great and final tension of the Cold War, and surely specific fears of nuclear war informed Wenders and Shepard as they directed Tom Farrell in the role of the screaming man (who improvised a part of this speech in a manner consistent with their wishes).

But of course nuclear annihilation is not the only form that the loss of a safety zone assumes. The screaming man may well be warning everyone that they are going to become adults, finally, irremediably, that the land of no return is the adult correlative to Neverland, where children never grow up. When we first reach the point of realizing the possibility of our own mortality, we come to be alone in a way that we never have before. This epistemological loneliness that reaches us upon adolescence is never quite shaken. How we negotiate its terrors is another question. But, to repeat myself, we are always facing the end of the world as we know it. If we fail to acknowledge our limitations we will be faced with a prophecy of doom, a constant confrontation with the nothingness that is the final end of the lonely self. The form our acknowledgment takes will shape how we are to live the rest of our lives.

At the conclusion of this speech Travis reaches out and touches the screaming man on the arm, as if to comfort him, but also as if to acknowledge that he has heard what has been said and will take it to heart. With such an understanding, he is finally equipped to acknowledge what he has previously avoided. That is, he is able to understand that he may not be able to accomplish a reunification of his family, that the circumstances of his life thus far, the terrible wound created by the force of his love for Jane and her reaction to it, will not heal. But there is another human being, Hunter, who needs to be considered, and it is in the end for him that the trip will be made.

This turn in the fate of Travis is not yet explicit. It will not become so until after his first sighting of Jane. But it is foreshadowed in that moment of the film, and from that moment on, following his encounter with the screaming man, Travis is able to begin to make a distinction that he was previously unable to make. When he sees Walt immediately after this scene, Walt is on a scaffold, putting up another billboard. He notices Travis's worried look and comments on Travis's fear of heights. This is when Travis corrects him, saying, "I'm not afraid of heights. I'm afraid of falling." At this moment Travis is able to realize that the objective world and his reaction to that world are two different things. He is, in short, stumbling upon Emerson's insight that the world he thinks and the world he converses in are not the same, and he is finally able to be true to that difference. In short, he is realizing the great lesson of experience, overcoming the condition that had led him to his lonely place. In his long walk Travis had tried to obliterate that distinction, and had come close to succeeding, but only by acting so as to risk hastening his death. But now he is someone else, a sojourner in life again, resigning himself to the condition of the human.

Paris, Texas ends simply. Hunter will begin his life with Jane. Travis will disappear again. Walt and Ann will go on with their lives. They, like us, will be extradited to the land of no return. But they are an imagined family, and their love is an imagined love. This ending is in its own way Lockean—the imagination of a clean slate, a child who will be raised to majority status, the good son. Out of the rubble of loss, a gain is made. And yet the screaming man reminds us that there is no return to a state of nature for us. Our mother, mother earth, will in her fury snatch us from our beds, heave us into the desert where we will wander. And we will look back and wonder if there ever was a time when it was better, whether that film within a film, the home movie with its brilliant 16-millimeter glow, conceals as much as it reveals.

Scene Two: The Keyhole Club

There is more to tell. I am drawn to the film *Paris, Texas* for other reasons, reasons shaped by memories of my own childhood. The film evokes for me some specific events of remembering and forgetting. While childhood may be presented as a strange pastoral, the innocence of halcyon days, even for as dark a thinker as Walter Benjamin,[7] this innocence is tinged by the rampaging forces of unlimited desire, by the stridency of temptation, by indignant rage. Hunter is aptly named, a not so innocent boy who seeks and finds his desire, the love of his mother. His quest for her could be read as a successful killing of his father, for in the end Travis is gone and Hunter has Jane to himself. And yet their work was collaborative, a triangle of love. Nothing is ever so simple as the simple fact of love.

In the lives of many of us, the question of the Oedipal framing of desire assumes a messier, less charged, but perhaps still determinative power. We love our mothers, perhaps especially when they are missing.

On a bright spring morning many years ago in a small city in western Pennsylvania, an exhausted mother of nine sat down at the kitchen table to have her mid-morning coffee and cigarette. She had just shooed her three youngest children out the door, and told the oldest of them, Tommy, a five-year-old boy, to watch his two-year-old sister and one-year-old brother as they played in a sandbox in the shade of a big maple tree in the backyard, right under the kitchen window. Tommy immediately began to dig into the sand, pretending that he was building a highway for his toy truck. His little sister, Therese, watched for a moment, and then started making a hill of sand with her shovel. After a while—it couldn't have been more than a minute or two—Tommy looked up and realized that baby Denny was missing. Out of the corner of his eye, he saw his little brother running as fast as a toddler can waddle, out of the yard and toward the street. Knowing his mom had put him in charge, Tommy ran after him, but by the time he reached the sidewalk, Denny was already in the street, plopped down in the middle of an intersection, crying his eyes out. The one thing Tommy knew was that it was strictly forbidden to go into the street. So from the

*edge of the sidewalk, as close as he could get to his brother, he yelled,
"Come here, Denny, come here!" But his brother didn't come. He
just sat there and wailed. To make matters worse, an old mangy
neighborhood dog named Buckets trotted out of the nearby alley, sat
down next to Denny, and began howling. Denny cried louder, and
then cars started coming down the street, stopped in front of the
spectacle, and honked their horns, as if that would get things moving. Tommy didn't know what to do, so he just kept calling to his
brother from the edge of the sidewalk.*

*Suddenly, as if out of nowhere, Tommy's oldest brother, Johnny,
an eighth grader who was on his way home from the nearby paro-
chial school for lunch, swooped down, picked Denny up in his arms,
and ran back to the house with him. The screen door banged shut.
And that is the last thing that Tommy remembers.*

When they were small, about the ages of Therese, Denny, and
Tommy, I would tell this story to my two children at bedtime. Our
family dog, Fred, would join us at the bedside, and when we reached
the point in the story when Denny cried and Buckets howled, we
all joined together, howling into the night. Buckets became in the
retelling a legendary, fierce, and savage wolf-dog, outwitted by my
heroic brother as he dashed down the street to rescue Denny. The
drama of Denny's escape, the terror of his older brother, Tommy,
the details of the street and the neighborhood would arrive with a
vividness unlike any other recollection of my childhood. In this retelling, the story became *Denny, Buckets, and the Amazing Rescue*. It
is a memory fragment as story.

Some of the story remains mysterious to me, or more accurately,
suspicious. What was my mother thinking that morning, leaving a
five-year-old in charge of two toddlers? Why don't I remember what
happened afterward at all, let alone with the same clarity as I do the
story itself? Is there simply a drive for narrative closure at work here,

or is the desire for closure a sign of something else inflecting my memory? There is an undercurrent of fear in my remembering, and a sadness about something lost from my childhood. This was not a happy family scene. It is easy to see now that my mother was suffering her own form of loneliness, that the pressure of bearing and caring for nine children in twelve years (plus having two miscarriages), of trying to manage the household while my father spent long days and nights selling life insurance, the crushing logistics of laundry, housecleaning, food preparation (for a number of years there were eleven people at the dinner table every day), bedtime, waking, preparing for school—all of this activity, with no other adult around all day long, took an enormous toll.

After her childbearing years had ended, my mother used to say that she missed being pregnant because that meant she would have a few days off in the hospital when it came time for delivery, a little postpartum vacation, where she could stay in bed all day while the nurses served her meals. With each new child her postpartum vacations seemed to become more protracted, her sorrow and anger more palpable, her time in bed upon returning home longer. After the childbearing years were over, she would sometimes retire to her bed for days at a time—to rest a bad back, it was said, a pinched nerve, a slipped disk. I've often wondered about that bad back.

One of the characteristics of our large family was that the further down the birth order (the pecking order) one was, the less attention was paid to the child. Our parents' professions of equal love for all were only as true as that is possible, which is to say, formally true, incidentally true, and over time substantively not so true. There were favorites—there had to be—and after the first three or four children, if the rest of us weren't replicas of the older ones, we certainly were diminished in comparison, slightly faulty clones. (We younger kids looked like the older ones; the older ones didn't look like us.) Our family photo albums reflected this inevitability. There were many pictures of my oldest sister, many of my oldest brother, and with each successive child, fewer and fewer, until a new flurry of photos cropped up after the last child arrived, as if they knew they were finally done. As the seventh of nine, I had, photographically speaking, an almost anonymous existence, appearing in a few group pictures, only posed alone once or twice, for instance, for my first communion, in the white suit and tie that symbolized my pure soul.

But I gathered attention, it seems, in other ways. My siblings have reminded me from time to time that I was a difficult child, prone to screaming fits, angry, bored, sharp-tongued, sometimes mean. I remember with great specificity my resentments and tantrums, my general sense of injustice, focused on the cruelties of my older siblings, cruelties that I transmitted downward in a concentrated fury onto my younger brother. I would retreat into books in the way of the alienated kid, reading the family encyclopedia, *Reader's Digest* condensed books, even the local newspaper, soon maxing out my public library card. I was called Foggy for my distracted air, sometimes affectionately, sometimes not. I was also called the runt of the litter—asthmatic, runny-nosed, scrawny, bespectacled, and foul-mooded, with more trips to the family doctor than my parents could afford. Another source of tension.

I remember the arguments of my mom and dad, the silences between them, the tension in the house, the accusatory tone in conversations at dinner, the anger in the air. Later in childhood, I came to love school, even school at Our Lady of Lourdes with the Sisters of Mercy, simply because I almost always knew where I stood with them, in a morally dubious hole, my besmirched soul in constant need of scrubbing. At home, I would never know what the mood would be. Especially as the older children left home, plunging into the turbulent world—serving as a nurse in Vietnam, joining the Peace Corps, protesting the war—their generational acts of rebellion against the political powers that be were read by my parents as personal offenses against them. A letter from the Philippines, a headline in the local paper about SDS at Penn State, a Walter Cronkite report on the evening news about the war—any one of these events could set off an explosion at the dining room table at home, where the remaining children would bear the brunt of our parents' anger at our older siblings.

Yet my troubles began before then, at home with my mother. I had a gnawing fear of her. She seemed to pay attention to me only when I caused trouble, so I guess I caused as much trouble as I could. When I threw tantrums, she would lock me away in a cubbyhole closet under the staircase in the dining room. But while I remember being locked up there for hours at a time, a part of me knows as well that it was never for that long, that it only felt that way at the time, and then forever after. The fact that I cannot remember what happened after my big brother John rescued Denny and took him inside the house tells me that something bad probably happened—a punishment, a humiliation, more tears, more hurt. Undoubtedly nothing out of the ordinary happened, as ordinary was defined in the household.

But these are love stories. There is more than a whiff of the erotic in my memory of this closet and my punishment there, the attention I received even as I was out of sight, my looking out into the light with one eye to the keyhole, looking for signs of my siblings going about their days, hidden, somehow protected as much as I was trapped. It is a feeling intense enough to reawaken my memory; I recall the vivid colors and pungent smells, the dust in the cubbyhole (where my mother's ironing board and vacuum cleaner were stored—the tools of the harried housewife). Every time I think I may lose this past, that faint smell of freshly ironed clothes, or the thrumming noise of the wind of a vacuum, assures me that I am in the world and reminds me that my past has led to this present. Like

Travis visiting the Keyhole Club in search of his lost wife, I return
to the scene of my love lost, to the mother who could not love me
and whom I learned not to love in return.

The smells of the cubbyhole, the light through the crack in the
door—these are the sensory cues that recall my own missing
mother. It is astonishing to realize that she has shaped the fact that I
write, that I think; that I look back now no longer in anger, but
with regret and a longing to re-imagine the way our family, any
family, might be able to work our way through the loneliness that
has saturated our existence together. This was her gift to me, to
launch me into the world I now inhabit, despite all else. From her I
first gained my sense of loneliness as a way of life.

My brothers and sisters are scattered across the continent, for
quite some time we were scattered across the world, but—with
some exceptions—we are closer together again as we age, as the oldest reach toward something called retirement. We sometimes blame
our scattering on the tumult of the times, each of us finding a different way to grow up in a wartime both foreign and domestic—
the politics of protest and vocations of humanitarian service, the
disastrous forays of some of us into drugs and alcohol as the decades followed each other—but it was also something else we fled,
and continue to flee.

My father still lives in our hometown, alone, mourning his wife
of more than fifty years, who died several years ago. (My mother finally received a diagnosis of clinical depression a week before she
died, too late for the antidepressants to kick in.) He and I get along
well, I think, bonded closer than some fathers and sons by the fact
of parallel losses. I call him every Sunday. We talk about politics,
the Pirates, the Red Sox, and Penn State football. I do not know
what he will think when he reads this chapter, because he is certain
that my mother was a wonderful mother, that her life was shaped
by being our mother, that she sacrificed for her children, and that

any other view of her life, the life of a mother who may have been missing, is simply unacceptable. He visits her grave every week, declining invitations to move to the towns of any of his children because he wants to stay close to her. I may not even tell him when this book is published, in part to spare him, in part because I still fear his anger, the residual power that a now sweet old man has over his prodigal son.

Each of my siblings has a memory, and each of us must remember our childhood differently. While some of us look back in anger, and others with regret, I know, I swear I know, that none of us look back with joy. But it is also true that none of us can claim to tell the story of our separate childhoods, our individual traumas, our lonely family, with a greater authority or a truth any more fundamental than the others. There are no experts when it comes to these questions of remembrance. We all recall from our own experience. We are separated by our common past.

How does a past such as this one inform the present? How do any of our memories of childhood refract themselves through the rest of our life? In our lengthy infancy, which is to say in our pre-philosophical days, long before that crucial moment when we first experience the existential terror that takes hold at adolescence, how are we able to make some separate sense of the world that would allow us to know it without giving in to our skepticism? Do we simply accept the fact that we each begin alone, for as long as we can remember, and not try to think again about our past? At the age of five we end our infancy and enter the beginning of high childhood, a late moment in many ways, already formed by what we cannot recall.

Which memories count? Which do not? These are the ties that bind us—the lonely family, the love lost, the harm we do to each other, the ways we try to overcome our selves, to rid ourselves of the past, even as we don't let go of it. On our deathbeds we will remember it all, it is said. Or, there will be a great forgetting, and only oblivion. As we look forward to that moment, we are also looking into our past, strung between two impossibilities, wondering at the sense of loss, wondering what, if anything, is to be gained by thinking about our lonely love. What we leave behind will be traces of our selves, worn through use, worn-out shoes, hieroglyphs for future archivists to puzzle over.

Chapter IV

Grieving

It is very unhappy, but too late to be helped, the discovery we have made, that we exist.

—Emerson

Sick World

In the spring of 1999, after a variety of tests and a first operation, my wife was diagnosed as suffering from a rare and terminal form of lung cancer called pleural mesothelioma. Subsequent experimental surgery that removed more of her insides than we thought possible, coupled with six months of the most intensive and hence brutal chemotherapy and radiation treatment available, extended her life for four and a half years. And we lived for a while as self-conscious exemplars of Kurt Vonnegut's "nation of two," bound closely together in the light of death's presence, constantly mindful of the impending event that would end our life in common. Sickness, remission, and recurrence moved us far from where we had been before that fatal diagnosis, first into a strange comedy of remarriage, then to the sorrow of anticipated grief with the cancer's return, and finally to facing the fateful contingencies of the final separation that

was to shape the remainder of my existence without her. Each surgery, each treatment, each new incursion of the cancer marked time
upon her body, the visible measure of time running out.

But in that period of remission we celebrated days of energy and
renewal, delighting in our still young children, happy to be bur-
dened by the blessed thoughtlessness of everyday concerns. We enjoyed as much as we could the many moments that became more
sharply focused in our ongoing encounter with the vivid knowledge
of a coming end.

When by myself, I sometimes would experience moments of
startling pain. A strange feeling would bubble up through my stom-
ach to my chest and throat. Blind reflection about the prospect of
her absence would take hold of me, and terror would overwhelm
me, a terror that I wished to be only about my love for her. But it
was also about her death and my survival, a confusion of fear and
dread that was to be a source of my befuddlement and anguish for
years to come. This sort of pain is only retrospectively explained
with reasons. To raise our children without her; to fear I could never
be loved by another, and to fear that I might; to be alone in an
empty house—these thoughts gather together to make up the cloy-
ing hurt of ordinary loss, the waking in the middle of the night,
hearing only more silence in the silence.

I would lose track of myself. Jogging on a bicycle trail near our
house one summer morning, I came to realize I was sobbing only
after being startled by the stares of others on the path, and so I
slowed to a walk to catch my breath, tears running down my face. I
was ashamed, realizing that I was grieving a loss that was not yet
mine to grieve.

There may be periods in one's life when the journey to death is
more pronounced as an event, if not because one senses sharply
one's own movement toward it, then because the atmosphere is
charged with news of dying as it occurs in others. In the period be-

fore my mother died, my father watched her final months of decline, caring for her, trying to help her, staying by her side and suffering with her. His lonely grief was already beginning as she slowly slipped away, as he moved her from their apartment into a nursing home when he could no longer meet the physical demands of her illness, and as she, depressed and frightened, slightly demented, shared her unhappiness in the bitter way of the unhappy old. Old, old, my parents in their eighties, bodies worn out by life, experiencing this final decline, what so many others have experienced through the ages.

Such encounters change us. How can they not? As these events unfolded in what was for me the middle of the decade of my forties, I found myself more comfortable in the company of older friends (both those who have aged before me and those who have aged with me), people who in the wake of my wife's diagnosis and treatment shared information about the various stages of their decrepitude, their cautious checking of blood sugar, pressure, and cholesterol levels, the results of examinations for colon, breast, prostate cancer, progress reports on the declining state of hearts, lungs, livers, backs, and knees, questionable Pap smears, strange lumps, failing sight. The heightened awareness of death and the betrayals of the body that we shared enabled my wife and me to notice how communities of the sick form around hospitals and their environments, extending their connections into homes and medicine cabinets and kitchens, how a heterotopia we sardonically called "sick world" shadows the world of health and seems at times to overtake the concerns of "well world."

Sick world, like all other worlds, has various rules of membership, initiation, and resignation. Almost everyone is familiar with sick world, though most of us hope to avoid it for as long as we can. It was only with this new appreciation of death-boundedness that we began to notice as a part of our everyday life what so many others have described in more rigorous and systematic ways—how the powers of the modern sciences of medicine allow not only the extension of life but a new kind of segregation of sickness from wellness and sick people from well people. The community of those who have nothing in common is made common to us through these modes of separation and uncommonness. Were we callous not to have noticed all of this before?

To have more time to think about death as one anticipates its approach may be a more common experience now than in the past—when infection surely and swiftly took us away—for those who live in technologically complex cultures. The life extenders of chemotherapy, coronary bypass surgery, angioplasty, and protease inhibitor regimens, the vaccines and antibiotics, and the other weapons of Western medicine have arrested or slowed the process of our dying, restoring, if in diminished states, many who otherwise would have gone to join the ranks of the dead. In thinking about the meaning of the experience of death-boundedness, I wonder how we might assess the difference this gift of technology makes. Does the thought of life extension offer up a hope that is false? Has it been only one more means of preventing us from getting closer to the reality of death? Or perhaps asking the question answers it—we are both emboldened to think anew and distracted from our thoughts, still left to our own devices after all is said and done. Or perhaps our new forms of evasion only reflect the oldest of our ruses of denial, the denial that allows us to continue to live.

These questions moved to the foreground the deeper we went into my wife's illness. Cancer is an illness that "progresses," and as Brenda's cancer progressed our sense of time shifted in new ways. A hesitation, a suspension of the moment, a stretching of time, an unease which is connected to the experience of boredom but which fills it so differently, a general mood of apprehension—all of these time bends are at work in the waiting rooms of hospitals, doctors'

offices, and psychotherapists' darkened dens. These are the spaces
where we focus on our losses. They are vestibules of time.

But our homes are otherwise. There, the clash of life surrounds
the paraphernalia of recovery and decline. In every home with a seriously sick person we find the debris of sickness—the clotted tis-
sues, the bedpans, the medicine bottles, heating pads, pillows and
reclining chairs, the oxygen machines and nasal tubes—residues of
the technologies brought to bear against the foreign agent, the failing part (in this case, one remaining, gradually collapsing lung).
These ordinary objects commingle with the newspapers and maga-
zines, the food in the refrigerator, the calendars of the children's
events, the blare of the television, the stacks of books, the needle-
point, the visitors, and cast a different light on the everyday life
of the household. We refashion our objects into waste, and may
find the waste more comforting, a way of healing the wounds, cov-
ering over the constitutive divisions between our bodies and our
minds. The home becomes a strangely comfortable jumble of life
and death.

Alphonso Lingis has written of the gradual withdrawal from the
world of those who are dying, their functions fading as they vacate
a space to be filled by others. The time of dying, he emphasizes, is
like no other time. "Dying takes time; it extends a strange time that
undermines the time one anticipates, a time without a future, without possibilities, where there is nothing to do but endure the presence of time. What is impending is absolutely out of reach."[1] As
we get closer to our death, the world begins to fall away and becomes less intelligible to us. Yet even as we withdraw from the
world, we become more intelligible to ourselves because we come
closer to experiencing what is beyond experience—not something
simply unknown, but that which is beyond the pairing of known
and unknown. Lingis teaches that we withdraw *from* the world and
into the world as death approaches. This falling from and into could

be called the loss of self, except that it is the most self-aware, most personal, most individuating moment of life, in which we become a member of the community of those who have nothing in common. "The shadow of death circumscribes, in the unending array of possibilities that are possible for anyone, what alone is possible for me" (169).

As the last sentence of his book on nothing, Lingis writes: "The grief, when the other has been taken and no medication or comfort were possible, understands that one has to grieve" (179). The nothing that grief teaches is that one has to grieve what is taken—not from me, or from you, only taken. The caregiver, soon to be the griever, goes toward the dying person to touch that person while she or he is still touchable, while that person is still capable of experiencing the comfort a touch may bring, while that person is still alive. "The touch of consolation is not itself a medication or protection; it is a solicitude that has no idea of what to do or how to escape . . . The touch of consolation is an accompaniment, by one mortal and susceptible to suffering, of the other as he sinks into the time that goes nowhere, not even into nothingness" (178). When that person is gone we grieve because, as Lingis knows, the lost one is no longer touchable.

Was that person ever touched? How can any one of us answer such a question? To experience the untouchable character of the death of someone we have touched and who has touched us is to experience the death of that person as an inverted form of birth. That which we imagine as a part of us is separate now; the separation is occasioned by the sinking into nowhere of the other. For Lingis, the imperative is found in the ethics of our responsible attention to the other in suffering and enjoyment. We may experience an enjoyment that is a consequence of how we embrace the imperative, how we trust our selves, how we notice the other. So often our lives turn around in moments when we are unaware of what we are doing. In this sense, more of life is retrospective than not. Shame comes to us when we reflect backward and see our failure to look forward. If the conditions of our possibility are known to us only retrospectively, then we are surely as lost as Lear, and not to be found again. To die out of nature, to enjoy ourselves, is to think forward, prospectively. Yet the final prospect for every one of us, and for those yet unborn, is the experience that leads to nothingness.

How, then, are we to live? In conversation, in comity, in the comedy of our hopelessness, we say. But what do we mean by such cheerful words in the face of death? How do we go on?

That we are death-bound is not news, and yet perhaps it is the most important news, the only news that matters. Most of the conversation about politics evades this thought, represses it in order to permit us to go about the business of killing time. We are also distracted from thinking about the meaning of loss when politics is concerned with victory after victory. The politics that distracts us from our existential concerns tends to undermine our common appreciation of the state of loneliness that comes upon us when others die to us, when our world is narrowed to its minimal possibilities, when we are alone in our grief. If we think about the experience of loss, the crossings of public and private that accompany the catastrophes humans suffer, the ways we attempt to evade or overcome or accept the disappearance of those we love, the turbulent reactions to loss which often replicate the circumstances of loss itself, we may sink into what seems an interminable analysis of our existence. But if we cannot reach a satisfactory resolution to mourning, we are nonetheless compelled to try to continue to live, which means learning to live with loss, living through disappearance. As we reckon our standing as grievers, we also give shape to particular ways of being in the world.

One way to imagine this reckoning is to note a peculiarity concerning the relationship of the grieving person to those who are not grieving. The simple and strangely brutal fact is that grieving is done by some in a larger world of many. The many can never note grief nor attend to it as the grievers do. Moreover, among grievers, each person grieves in a highly individualized way, as a father, or mother, or child, or spouse, or friend of the person who has died. It is not that there are so many other people who do not share in our experience; the truth is that almost everyone does, at some time, go through grieving. Rather, it is the world itself that turns against us when we experience such a loss. The sun still shines, the birds still sing, as W. E. B. Du Bois noted of the day his son died. Life goes on, and we who grieve are bewildered and incredulous that this death is happening, has happened, and that no one else is feeling it as we are feeling it, that it is not fully registered by the calendar of the world. When we are struck by grief, we are led to a certain form of disbelief, to attending to the rest of the world as if it has become unreal. Our efforts to reclaim perspective may be frustrated by the very strangeness of the world itself.[2] This mismatch between world and self looms large at such times, and the fact that the world actually is full of both terrible and sublimely beautiful things, people, and events makes the path of grief more tortuous.

And yet there is still a connection between personal grief and the world at large. How one describes that connection is a difficult matter, for there is never a simple connection between self and world, between private and public. Perhaps the problem can be illustrated by posing a few questions. For instance: what difference, if any, did it make that my wife began her dying as the George W. Bush administration launched a preemptive war against Iraq, as the national mood turned from the unreality of mourning to an odd exaltation after a faux victory lap by an increasingly arrogant executive, and then turned bitter and sour as the mounting death toll and multiple scandals of corruption and incompetence revealed that same man's malice? Did the strange national spasm of a war and the ensuing domestic divisions in the United States reflect or intensify the process of dying that was occurring in our household? Would it even be possible to claim that a better death might await us in times of peace than in times of war? Somehow the answer to this last question ought to be yes, but it is no simple matter to explain why that should be the case.

Our lonely way of being connects the innermost to the outermost, the personal to the political, and the trauma of individuals to the formation of the state in strange and attenuated ways, which by dint of their very thinness emphasize the powers of our connections to each other. By engaging the subject of mourning, by reflecting on ways in which the path from the individual to the collective seems to transform mourning into a form of collective melancholia, perhaps we learn more about the pathos of loneliness: the path of loneliness in grieving leads us to the community of those who have nothing in common. Perhaps as well we may glimpse an alternative to, or another imagining of, how we are to absorb our losses.

We have models before us to explore—Sigmund Freud's demand for a disillusionment with the human, and Judith Butler's plea for an adherence to a Levinasian ethics as ways to negotiate our way through loss. Yet another imagining of our way forward is found for me in Emerson, who seems both to embody the melancholia described by Freud and Butler and yet points us to an alternative re-membering of the traumatic body politic. But even if Emerson moves us forward in one way, we may need to move in another way as well, to a recognition of the struggle of those successors to Antigone and Pip, those abject subjects who are denied what we may call the right to mourn. This is where Du Bois provides us with a strange solace.

To outline this perilous path of grief, its irresolution, and the danger of unresolved grief may seem to be a foolish enterprise. Better simply to live, we might say, better simply to move from dream to dream. But I think that to pursue grief through to its end may lead to something else, to a turn away from the interminable, or perhaps more precisely, to use a phrase from Du Bois, to a hope not hopeless, yet not hopeful.

The Invention of Ghosts

How do we tell where we are on the path of grief? The boundary lines seem clearly demarcated, but appearances can be deceiving. Early in his classic 1917 essay "Mourning and Melancholia," Freud claims that "mourning is regularly the reaction to the loss of a loved person, or the loss of some abstraction which has taken the place of one, such as fatherland, liberty, an ideal, and so on."[3] This sentence, seemingly straightforward, ends up entangling us in a complex set of connections—to lose a person, to lose a fatherland, to lose a liberty, to lose an ideal. It is important to keep in mind Freud's elision of person to fatherland, liberty, and ideal as we examine his argument concerning the divergent dynamics of mourning and melancholia, because our fullest understanding of mourning depends upon it.

In his initial thoughts on the subject, Freud describes melancholia as a flawed version of mourning. While mourning is a reaction to the loss of a loved one, at least in this essay Freud considers it to be a process that, albeit painfully, eventually reaches some sort of resolution. "The task is carried through bit by bit, under great expense of time and cathectic energy, while all the time the existence of the lost object is continued in the mind. Each single one of the memories and hopes which bound the libido to the object is brought up and hyper-cathected, and the detachment of the libido from it accomplished . . . The fact is, however, that when the work of mourning is completed the ego becomes free and uninhibited again" (154). Such grief work takes time—the grieving person may think he is free when he is only coming up for air. He may imagine himself to be over his grief only to have it hit him again, from a different angle of experience. And yet there comes a time when he is free. Or so Freud suggests in this essay.

In contrast, for the melancholiac no such journey to detachment occurs. Instead, on the surface at least, the melancholiac experiences an extraordinarily intense wave of guilt and self-abasement, an experience that is carried out, interestingly enough, in a public way.

> It must strike us that after all the melancholiac's behavior is not in every way the same as that of one who is normally devoured by remorse and self-reproach. Shame before others, which would characterize this condition above everything, is lacking in him, or at least there is little sign of it. One could almost say that the opposite trait of insistent talking about himself and the pleasure in the consequent exposure of himself predominates in the melancholiac. (157)

Freud suggests that the clinical picture the melancholiac presents is that of someone whose "self-reproaches are actually reproaches against a loved object which have been shifted onto the patient's own ego" (158). Melancholiacs lack shame, he believes, because their self-plaints are actually not directed against themselves, but at someone else.

But who is this someone else? It turns out that this other self is the lonely self—still our own self, but the self we hate to be. Freud understands the plunge into melancholia as akin to narcissism.

> First there existed an object-choice, the libido had attached itself to a certain person; then, owing to a real injury or disappointment concerned with the loved person, this object-relationship was undermined. The result was not the normal one of withdrawal of the libido from this object and transference of it to a new one, but something different for which vari-

ous conditions seem to be necessary. The object-cathexis proved to have little power of resistance, and was abandoned; but the free libido was withdrawn into the ego and not directed to another object. It did not find application there, however, in any one of several possible ways, but served simply to establish an *identification* of the ego with the abandoned object. Thus the shadow of the object fell upon the ego, so that the latter could henceforth be criticized by a special mental faculty like an object, like the forsaken object. In this way the loss of the object became transformed into a loss in the ego, and the conflict between the ego and the loved person transformed into a cleavage between the criticizing faculty of the ego and the ego as altered by the identification. (159)

The ego thus is split—in the form of the "special mental faculty" which is like an object (but which is actually an aspect of the ego). This special mental faculty criticizes the ego for the harm it has done to the object, but it also identifies with the lost object, having incorporated the loved object into the ego as a loss of self.

Freud suggests that this ego identification is narcissistic in its structure and dynamic. But it is triggered by a loss, and thus it at least borrows from the process of grief. What happens in the face of the trauma of loss is that the deep structural ambivalence in love-relationships comes to the fore. This ambivalence emerges in the grieving process as well as in melancholia; it occurs when there is the presence of *any* disposition toward obsessional neurosis. This is a rather common human condition, and it is also a condition that practically defines grief. For the melancholiac, however, this condition of ambivalence is both broader—in that there are losses other than death that can occasion the downward slide—and somehow deeper—in that the conflict of ambivalence is transferred onto the melancholiac's ego, which becomes the substitute object for the missing loved one. "If the object-love, which cannot be given up, takes refuge in narcissistic identification, while the object itself is abandoned, then hate is expended upon this new substitute-object, railing at it, depreciating it, making it suffer and deriving sadistic gratification from its suffering. The self-torments of melancholiacs, which are without doubt pleasurable, signify, just like the corresponding phenomenon in the obsessional neurosis, a gratification of sadistic tendencies and of hate, both of which relate to an object and in this way have both been turned around upon the self" (161–162). We turn to hate because the object of our love has left us alone, has abandoned us to our selves, and our selves are empty, lonely. Even more, our selves as our love-objects are not worthy of our selves. How can they be? They are not loved. The core paradox of the melancholiac involves an unwillingness to accept the self as worthy of love, especially love by one's own self.

This turning to hate may in fact explain suicide. "Now the analysis of melancholia shows that the ego can kill itself only when, the object-cathexis having been withdrawn upon it, it can treat itself as an object, when it is able to launch against itself the animosity relating to an object—that primordial reaction on the part of the ego to all objects in the outer world" (162–163). This turning is explained in the essay "Instincts and Their Vicissitudes." Crudely put, it is there that Freud establishes the priority of hate over love in the formation of the ego—his original explanation for the ambivalence of love.[4] When we hate, we become objects to ourselves, and suicide becomes a pleasure.

Thus, the deepest problem of melancholia is that there is a regression of libido into the ego, brought about by the ego identification as a way of coping with the loss of the loved object. Freud suggests that of the three conditioning factors in melancholia—loss of the object, ambivalence, and regression of libido into the ego—it is the third that is unique to melancholia. He concludes this essay by saying, "That accumulation of cathexis which is first of all 'bound' and then, after termination of the work of melancholia, becomes free and makes mania possible, must be connected with the regression of the libido into narcissism. The conflict in the ego, which in melancholia is substituted for the painful struggle surging round the object, must act like a painful wound which calls out unusually strong anti-cathexes" (169–170). In other words, we pick and pick and pick—we return to the site of loss, we can't believe it, we are incredulous to our selves, we are permanently injured. We are, in short, lost to ourselves, and we spend our time hopelessly searching for what has disappeared.

It is true that Freud later softened the distinction between the states of grief and melancholia, suggesting that the grieving subject may never completely detach himself from the lost object, that the grieving subject may indeed experience an ambivalence in reference to the next object to which he attaches himself.[5] Nonetheless, it may still be useful for us to ask what these unusually strong anti-cathexes may be composed of. Here I think we may, with some license from Freud, observe that 1917, the year "Mourning and Melancholia" was written, was a war year. Freud has many things to say about how war has an impact on our attitudes of love and hate, noting particularly how the dynamics of hate and sadism relate to our attitudes toward death. In another essay written in 1915, he is dramatic in presenting his early understanding of this connection.

The essay, "Thoughts for the Times on War and Death," contains a speculation (anticipating some of his observations in *Totem and Taboo* and *Civilization and Its Discontents*) that relates the emergence of self-consciousness in ancient man to the death of a very unusual enemy—the one who is loved by he who has killed him.

> Man could no longer keep death at a distance, for he had tasted
> of it in his grief for the dead; but he still could not consent en-
> tirely to acknowledge it, for he could not conceive of himself

as dead. So he devised a compromise; he conceded the fact of death, even his own death, but denied it the significance of annihilation, which he had no motive for contesting where the death of his enemy had been concerned. During the contemplation of his loved one's corpse he invented ghosts, and it was his sense of guilt at the satisfaction mingled with his sorrow that turned these new-born spirits into evil, dreaded demons. The changes wrought by death suggested to him the disjunction of the individuality into a body and a soul—first of all into several souls; in this way his train of thought ran parallel with the process of disintegration which sets in with death. The enduring remembrance of the dead became the basis for assuming other modes of existence, gave him the conception of life continued after apparent death.[6]

From this moment of the birth of religious belief Freud traces "the earliest inkling of ethical law" in the prohibition: Thou shalt not kill. This prohibition "was born of the reaction against the hate-gratification which lurked behind the grief for the loved dead, and was gradually extended to unloved strangers and finally even to enemies."

Once upon a time we lived with our ghosts, we kept them in valued places as reminders of our vulnerabilities. They were helpmeets in our moral progress even as we feared their demonic presence in our lives. But World War I, Freud suggests, has shown that "this final extension is no longer experienced by civilized man."[7] We no longer value our ghosts. Instead, our own existence has become ghostly; we have come to haunt ourselves.

This failure to extend a sense of love and dread marks for Freud a turning point in the development of humanity, what we might imagine as a shift from the possibility of a collective form of mourning to a narcissistic mode of melancholia. The problem is less that we have failed to extend the ethic universally than it is that the original impulse has reached a termination point because our ghosts have become exhausted. Our ghosts are exhausted because their power is no longer recognized by us as we turn away from the task of humanization and instead engage, in Judith Butler's terms, in a discourse that is both silent and melancholic.[8] Our silence signifies the depth of our loneliness. To recognize our ghosts would be to renew our respect for the process of grieving, rather than to truncate it, to ignore even their exhausted presence among us.

Despite what so many have accused him of doing, Freud did not map individual psychology onto the social in any reductive or simple way. In fact, he was deeply suspicious of the possibility of untangling the individual from the collective, even as he tried to do so in order to see more clearly the ways in which the two were connected. What still and always must be tested is whether and how the psychoanalytic technique, a technique that relies upon a counter-ruthlessness in the quest for a self-knowledge of our deepest impulses, is up to the task of breaking our pathology of melancholia; whether the psychoanalytic exercise is doomed to failure because it is unable to overcome our narcissistic resistance to the truth. Here is where a turn to the politics of identification may be of some use.

Undone by Each Other

In "Violence, Mourning, Politics," one of her reflections on the consequences of 9/11 for American society gathered in the volume *Precarious Life,* Judith Butler suggests something like the idea of the exhaustion of ghosts, almost as a side observation concerning the obituary as a form of public grieving. While she is most concerned about the impossibility of writing an obituary for the enemy, she is also aware of the difficulty of public grieving more generally, and sees the obituary as playing a crucial role in establishing the possibility of a grievable life.

[The obituary] is the means by which a life becomes, or fails to become, a publicly grievable life, an icon for national self-recognition, the means by which a life becomes note-worthy. As a result, we have to consider the obituary as an act of nation-building. The matter is not a simple one, for, if a life is not grievable, it is not quite a life; it does not qualify as a life and is not worth a note. It is already the unburied, if not the unburiable. (34)

In mentioning the unburiable, Butler's implicit reference seems to be to Antigone, and to the suspension between life and death that is the unhappy state of the unburied. In this passage she seems to suggest that our ghosts are exhausted to the extent that they remain among us, to the extent that we refuse to bury them.

Butler argues that grief is unavoidably a public phenomenon. Like Freud, she understands that the sense of loss can be attached not only to a person, but to the loss of a place and a community. But she purposely entangles the psychoanalytic with the social, with an immediate forcefulness that complicates Freud's understanding of extension. She notes that even when we are thinking and conversing at the most simple social level of a dyad, there is always a broader social context within which we understand our loss, a context that ultimately determines the composition of our being.

It is not as if an "I" exists independently over here and then simply loses a "you" over there, especially if the attachment to "you" is part of what composes who "I" am. If I lose you, under these conditions, then I not only mourn the loss, but I become inscrutable to myself. Who "am" I, without you? . . . At another level, perhaps what I have lost "in" you, that for which I have no ready vocabulary, is a relationality that is composed neither

exclusively of myself nor you, but is to be conceived as *the tie* by
which those terms are differentiated and related. (22)

For Butler, this "relationality" is how grief is politicizing, how it
brings to the fore the ties that bind us to one another. In grief, these
ties are revealed most fully in their brokenness. As she eloquently
puts it, "Let's face it. We're undone by each other. And if we're not,
we're missing something" (23).

This thought concerning the relation of each person to the other
raises difficult questions about how to engage each other politically, questions that come to the fore in moments of grief. For instance, how do we acknowledge our fundamental dependency on
others within the context of political rights discourse, which depends upon ideas of bodily integrity and self-determination? The
paradox is a deep one, because the demands of embodiment sometimes invoke our need not only to think about mortality, vulnerability, touch, violence, and risk, but to acknowledge how the body
bridges the public/private gap. As Butler puts it, "Constituted as
a social phenomenon in the public sphere, my body is and is not
mine. Given over from the start to the world of others, it bears their
imprint, is formed within the crucible of social life; only later, and
with some uncertainty, do I lay claim to my body as my own, if, in
fact, I ever do" (26).

Grief sets in motion the idea of our dispossession from ourselves.
But rather than being possessed by others, in this form of dispossession we move in an errant and uncharted direction. So we attempt
to rein in our grief. Reinforced by the culture of possession, our
grief thus gives rise to some of the most potent defenses against its
power. While the denial of the sentence of death that accompanies
a terminal diagnosis is a prime example of such a defense, the power
of denial as it moves to the public realm of trauma takes on the eerie, ghostly form of disembodiment. Those powers that insist upon
disembodiment as the proper form that political life must take cor-

relate with a kind of liberalism of the open mind/closed body, in Anne Norton's analysis.[9] When we are disembodied as political beings, the very form of our politics will not allow the work of grief to be completed but instead will interdict that work, turning it to other ends. It is those other powers that have dominated the world of the lonely self, ordering our priorities, separating us in the name of uniting us.

Butler usefully observes several of the commentaries that loomed large immediately following 9/11: William Safire citing Milton, that we must banish melancholy; President Bush announcing on 9/21 that we have finished grieving, and that we must replace grieving with resolute action (29). Her citation of these comments is in the service of pointing out not only how we come to fear the power of grief, but also how the blocking of grieving, the repression of grief, may lead to a fantasy of a return to orderliness, to a clean and completed grieving—something that itself is a matter to be resisted if we are in any meaningful way to address the world that has inflicted this harm upon us. (This fantasy is all the more potent when coupled with the claim that 9/11 has changed everything, that there is no going back to the way things were before. For the grieving person, this is inevitably true, but the way that we comprehend this changed state of being is, of course, the crux of the matter. The call by President Bush immediately after the attack that we should resume consuming, gather more possessions, is a piece of this puzzle as well.)

Butler asks if there would not be something to be gained by grieving, "from remaining exposed to its unbearability and not endeavoring to seek a resolution of grief through violence." She asks, "Could the experience of a dislocation of First World safety not condition the insight into the radically inequitable ways that corporeal vulnerability is distributed locally?" To engage in this kind of grieving, she suggests, would be to "develop a point of identification with suffering itself" (30).

While this plea may sound naïve to our jaded ears, it prefaces an intense discussion of the dire alternative, namely the dehumanization that is the result of the prohibition of certain kinds of public grieving. Noting the hierarchies of humanity that are implicit in the grieving of "our" lives versus those of others, Butler sees the path toward dehumanization as beginning from the very failure to tarry over grief. But more, those who are known to be ungrievable remain unburied for us. They are akin to Polyneices, Antigone's brother. If Antigone's assertion of her power to grieve was to raise questions about what constitutes legitimate love, then what may be the range of claims to a kinship between living and dead available to us *now* that would help us overcome the delimitations of the national state of suspended grief? In her brilliant reading in *Antigone's Claim*, Butler suggests that Antigone may in fact represent a sort of fateful conjoining of gender and national melancholia, the melancholia that emerges when the subject is in a deep condition of ambivalence concerning the lost love object. This ambivalence, for Butler, is the result of the strange relation that Antigone has with Oedipus, her brother-father, and Polyneices, her brother-nephew. She suggests that Antigone herself may best be comprehended as "the occasion of a new field of the human, achieved through political catachresis, the one that happens when the less than human speaks as human, when gender is displaced, and kinship founders on its founding laws."[10]

Thus Butler is able to see how significant the interdiction of certain kinds of mourning is in our present circumstances. Dehumanization, she suggests, emerges at the limits of discursive life; it is constituted as "a refusal of discourse that produces dehumanization as a result" (36). She writes,

> It seems important to consider that the prohibition on certain forms of public grieving itself constitutes the public sphere on the basis of such a prohibition. The public will be created on

the condition that certain images do not appear in the media, certain names of the dead are not utterable, certain losses are not avowed as losses, and violence is derealized and diffused. (37–38)

Butler notes that the immediate effect of these prohibitions is to shore up nationalism, but that another effect is the creation of a new kind of national subject, a "sovereign and extra-legal subject, a violent and self-centered subject" (41). The constitution of a public sphere on the ground of such an interdiction of discourse on the appropriate objects of mourning transforms the mourning subject into a melancholic one—a subject engaged in a national narcissistic quest for perfect security. And so we claim that we will fight and win a war on a concept—terror—and cannot admit to ourselves how absurd such an assertion is. But to fight such a war somehow feels better than facing the truth of our loss.

Butler's response to the trap of national narcissism is to turn to what she perceives to be the most specific and concrete ways of thinking about others, namely, an ethics of faciality, borrowed from the thought of Emmanuel Levinas. This response, I believe, is a dangerous one, because in Levinasian ethics an appreciation of attenuating circumstances, the articulation of the incomplete and open, in the end gives way to an exclusive recapitulation of the human, so that what appears to be other than human still comes to appear as less than human. In other words, there seems to be a regression from the stance toward the human that appears in Butler's original reading of Antigone. This recapitulation, however sensitive to the demands of a way of being, fails to register the political claim of those who are not already reckoned as human. Of course, this problem may reflect the risk present in the assertion of any and all ethics. But it is also possible that there is another path to the more open position Butler seeks than through the thought of Levinas.

A turning point occurs in Butler's gloss on Levinas's concept of faciality, from which the core ethical demand of his philosophy emerges. The face does not speak, but it nonetheless means, and what it means is the commandment, "Thou shalt not kill" (132). (This source of the commandment is more primal in some ways than is Freud's suggestion concerning the origins of the ethical imperative, but it is also, perhaps, more limiting.) With Levinas, Butler suggests that it is crucial that this command be comprehended as at least in part a result of the unspeaking character of the face and its extension through a catachresis to the neck, to the throat, to the back, "or indeed, just a mouth or a throat from which vocalizations emerge that do not settle into words" (133). The wordless vocalizations of suffering make us subject to the absolute demand of the other. We are to understand peace, in Levinas's words, as "an awakeness to the precariousness of the other" (134). This peace, it should be emphasized, extends to all others, and is based upon an insistent demand that comes from a not exclusively human face.

While we may applaud this sensitivity—how are we to oppose such a demand?—it is important to note as well how this catachresis differs in scale from the catachresis that Butler defends in *Antigone's Claim*. In the case of Antigone, there is a specificity of circumstance in her claim for a foundering founding, for a dissettling of engenderment, and for the emergence of a new field of the human. The non-human element in the faciality that Levinas elevates to the status of being an absolute principle seems to be simply asserted, not shown. Indeed, the claims of the face and voice in Levinas remain human in their scale. In contrast to the deeply situated Antigone, whose complex kinship becomes the site of a social contestation, the social itself recedes in Levinas, absorbed into the demands of an absolute responsibility that dissolves paradox. In contrast, Antigone embraces a paradox of a specific sort—we cannot help acting in a specific circumstance, moving forward despite the precariousness of life. On the other hand, if we are to attend to the precariousness of life through the mediation of the faciality of the other, then how do we get to the point of that more global recognition without moving through the field of action? Levinasian ethics seems to count on a pre-given inclination to a global unbidden, to a great unknown. That unknown takes the form of Yahweh, of the voice that gives us the word of God. In the end, it is as if that voice, the voice of God, becomes the only voice that matters—as if Levinas in the end is reduced to the position of his greatest protagonist, Heidegger, who in his final interview claimed that "only a God can save us now."

Butler takes the force of this criticism, but still embraces the need for an absolute responsibility to inform a specifically Jewish ethic of nonviolence despite the dangerous possibilities of another exclusion that it presents. I think that she does so because she understands the Levinasian ethic to express the paradox of representation at this most important general level: "For representation to convey the human, then, representation must not only fail, but it must *show* its failure. There is something unrepresentable that we nevertheless seek to represent, and that paradox must be retained in the representation we give" (144). Butler thus embraces the idea of retaining the paradox as the core ethical task.

But is retaining the paradox a *task* as much as it is an *acknowledgment* of the existential circumstances in which we find ourselves? In other words, are we retaining this paradox through our acts of representation, or is representation itself paradoxical in structure? It may be the case that what is at stake in such an ethics is no more than a heightened awareness of our common reliance upon language, even at the limits of language. And if that is so, then the embrace of paradox is only a starting point at best, or a spinning of our ethical wheels at worst.

In another sense, to sustain an ethic on the basis of the paradox of representation may not be possible as a task in and of itself, and hence if it is to be presented as the most prominent alternative to the powers of national melancholia, we may risk enfolding the specific tasks that are involved in becoming human into the transcendental powers of a sort of Hegelian overcoming. This is the deepest of all transcendental temptations, that they may in the end only replicate the narcissism of the human at a higher level of abstraction. It is not the deepest impulse that informs Butler's thought or work, but it remains a temptation to all of us, to seek some resting point, however precarious, from which we may make a claim upon the world, to be good without succumbing to a moralistic set of rules, avoiding a command while responding to an imperative to become as human as we may.

So what are we to do if we suspect that the Levinasian project in the end reverts to this deeply intractable problem of narcissism that so concerned Freud? What claims can we make that may be more akin to the radical claim of Antigone than the ethics of Levinas? What might seem to be the unpromising ground of the American experience may, surprisingly, provide another beginning point from which to move through our grief, to something like a new birth—and in that new birth, to experience an attenuation of our grief.

"I grieve that grief can teach me nothing"

If Freud and Butler seek to explain the experience of loss and to work through its pathology, Emerson moves immediately to a more complex problem, a problem toward which they both direct us: how we are to feel the loss of something in a world that is already lost to us? This is actually the question concerning the possibilities of conversion—whether it is possible for us to change, to become something other than what we already are. Emerson's answer, to paraphrase Stanley Cavell, is to establish finding as founding. In

this sense, Emerson may afford us an alternative sense of the openness of the world as a place of becoming, a place for the realization
of what he once referred to as the unattained but attainable self. For
Emerson, openness is achieved through the abandonment of what
is otherwise to be conserved, namely, the form of personality that is
at the heart of the psychic life of power.

Emerson's starting point in his argument concerning the politics
of grief is the assertion that grief is to be the ground condition of
the *beginning* of experience. He shocks his readers by comparing
the death of his son Waldo to a bankruptcy of his debtors, claiming
that the loss of property entailed by their failure to pay him might
inconvenience him but would

> leave me as it found me,— neither better nor worse. So it is
> with this calamity: it does not touch me: some thing which I
> fancied was a part of me, which could not be torn away without
> tearing me nor enlarged without enriching me, falls off from
> me, and leaves no scar. It was caducous.[11]

These sentences have been a source of great controversy. How cruel
of him, how cold he must be, say some. Others have suggested that
it is his very depth of feeling that leads him to describe his numbness, his shock. There is more here, however. In this section of the
essay "Experience," especially in two sentences that frame this observation (two of Emerson's most mysteriously truthful sentences),
he is thinking about the possibility of grief itself. A sentence after:
"I grieve that grief can teach me nothing, nor carry me one step
into real nature." A page before: "The only thing that grief has
taught me is how shallow it is" (472). In both of these sentences
grief is paradoxically proposed as its lack, as a lesson not to be
learned, as a shallow appearance. And this lesson of lack is connected to all of experience.

More specifically, the clause "I grieve that grief can teach me nothing" is deeply ambiguous. On the one hand, it suggests that grief is useless, in the sense that it is impossible to learn anything from grief. Taken that way, it proposes a paradox in the form of what appears to be an oxymoron. If grief is useless, why does one grieve, even if only to grieve the uselessness of grief? To grieve that one grieves is only to compound the uselessness of the process. But this may be the point, that a true depth of feeling concerning the uselessness of grief leads us to the shallows of all representations, and this is the way we lead ourselves to a fuller sense of uselessness. Reaching that sense of uselessness may be a first step into moving forward, finding a grounding to persist in our existence. This is an alternative way of thinking of the paradox of representation itself.

On the other hand, the phrase suggests that grief can teach us *about* nothing. In this case, we are grieving the learning of nothing-ness, the death-bounded journey to nowhere. When the phrase is parsed this way, we learn that to grieve that grief can teach me nothing may mean that I am sorry for the knowledge that constitutes my fall into the realization that I am human and finite, the realization that I am to die one day, that in the end there is nothing to look forward to but death. Yet the lesson of nothing, as we already know from Cordelia's father, is that nothing comes of nothing. We must speak again. Because this Emersonian sentence already speaks to us twice, we are on our way into a pedagogy of grief, an elemental learning experience.

There are different ways through this pedagogy of grief. One way is to ask what it means to take a step or to be carried a step into real nature. Then one might think back to Emerson's opening lines of "Experience," asking where we find ourselves, and answering that we find ourselves in a series, on a stair. We might note that the term "series" suggests the writing of a philosophy in a series of essays, the subject of which is to be the very possibility of writing one's experience, of writing one's philosophy.[12] We might note as well that at

the heart of this essay, Emerson comments that when he is thinking, conversing with a profound mind, he becomes apprised of his
"vicinity to a new and excellent region of life."

> By persisting to read or to think, this region gives further sign
> of itself. But every insight from this realm of thought is felt as
> initial, and promises a sequel. I do not make it; I arrive there,
> and behold what was there already. I make! O no! I clap my
> hands in infantine joy and amazement, before the first opening
> to me of this august magnificence, old with the love and hom-
> age of innumerable ages, young with the life of life, the sun-
> bright Mecca of the desert. And what a future it opens! I feel a
> new heart beating with the love of the new beauty. I am ready
> to die out of nature, and be born again into this new yet unap-
> proachable America I have found in the West. (485)

This finding, this founding, is to be a departure from nature that
comes from grief even as it overcomes it. It is taking steps in experience, away from the deadness of thoughtlessness and into the action of thinking. It is also a realization of what it might mean to
think of something as unapproachable, and hence points us toward
a never to be completed project of rebirth and renewal. This is Emerson's claim for philosophy in America, an America that is unapproachable, to be found(ed) again, renewed every day, democrati-
cally amended as we will it to change through the diurnal turnings
of each and every one of us.

America as an unknowable destination is the open grounding
that Emerson provides for thinkers who want to stake a new claim
for overcoming loss. In this new yet unapproachable America we
are to embrace a humanity where we find it, in the comings and
goings of our fellow citizens. The realization of our selves can only
occur through this openness, through a willingness to claim experience for our selves by way of both an aversion to conformity, that

deadness that permits us not to think, and a recognition of the power of our thinking selves to connect to others by way of our common understanding of the grounding of actions. For all of us, this America is to become a place from which we might move forward, and also a place we may turn toward, a province of life to which we may re-sign ourselves after our departure, and hence be ever able to act together and apart. The realization of this world through the experience of openness is enabling. We move; thought becomes an action. Thinking *is* an action of becoming.

But we may object to this idea as not affording a way of reflecting upon the past and hence becoming whole. Such movements may be good for our morale—and such a therapeutic result should not be underestimated—but they do not seem to aid us in understanding how we are to re-member the past. Remembering is a key trope for Emerson. But Emerson's play with the relationship between experience and experimentation in another important essay, "Circles," seemingly leads away from remembering and in another direction when he writes:

> But lest I should mislead any when I have my own head and obey my own whims, let me remind the reader that I am only an experimenter. Do not set the least value on what I do, or the least discredit on what I do not, as if I pretended to settle any thing as true or false. I unsettle all things. No facts to me are sacred; none are profane; I simply experiment, an endless seeker with no Past at my back.[13]

In "Circles" the presence of the present and its opening to the future seem to leave almost no room for an invocation of the past. This sense of overwhelming presence is reinforced in yet another essay by Emerson, "The American Scholar," when he writes, "Give me insight into today and you may have the antique and future worlds."[14] This passage is an indicator of how Emerson addresses the tragedy of a diminished past and an unknown future—not by repudiating the relationships of the past and future to the present, but by telling us that we may re-member the past through a constant and true fidelity to the present, a present that we may (or may not) overcome in a future as yet unmarked.

What means are available to us to overcome this relentless present, this aphasia that seems to prevent us from learning from experience? Turning to the epochal for the meaning it may provide is one common resolution of the paradox of presentism. This would, however, be another way of succumbing to the temptation for a settled ethics, a fulcrum from which to lever the world. Another way would be to emphasize the impersonal, a dissolution of personhood as a means, if not of overcoming the numbness of grief, then of accepting the loss of others as a means of losing oneself as well. An alternative way of taking steps in the pedagogy of grief, complementary to Emerson's turn toward this new yet unapproachable America, would be to develop a fuller understanding of what it might mean to be untouched. For the ability to skim the surfaces and allow them to provide a grounding from which we may act is complemented by our ability to overcome our disability of being untouched. This would be to vacillate between the personal and the impersonal, a way of proceeding that is illuminated by the claim in "Experience" that "We thrive by casualties. Our chief experiences have been casual" (483).

But let us look more closely at the question of touch. Emerson claims that the calamity of the death of his son leaves him untouched, with no scar. "It was caducous," he writes. It falls away from him, and there is no sign that his son was ever there in the first place. Emerson is untouched, and in being untouched he is untouchable. The untouchable is a figure of isolation, of absolute loneliness. As with Lingis, for whom the touching of the dying is the essence of an errant and yet essential humanity, for Emerson the touch is both necessary for us to become actors in the world of experience and yet inevitably and unavoidably an impossible act. Another clue to the meaning of being untouched is provided in Emerson's seemingly offhand observation in "Experience": "Was it Boscovich who found that bodies never come in contact? Well, souls never touch their objects" (473). "Touch" is a word that comes from the old French *toucher*, which is related to the Italian *tocco*, to knock, stroke, and *toccare*, to strike or hit, both of which emphasize the violence of contact. The violence of touch, the contact with corporeality, is a refusal by the Emersonian soul, a refusal that may be overcome in some other place, in some other way, perhaps by someone else. Touching contains within it an entire critique of Descartes; it is a force that makes us confront the fact of our mortality, our need for each other, and, as Butler puts it, the fact that we are undone by each other. (For me, the violence of touch is most clearly addressed from within the space created by Michel Foucault's lingering attachment of the soul to the body in *Discipline and Punish*.)

The two observations, the first concerning the caducous character of his loss—the calamity of his son's death—and the second regarding the strange "fact" of souls never touching their objects, might be seen as adumbrating Emerson's transcendentalist understanding of the fate of spirit in the play of philosophical understanding. "Caducous" means the falling off of a limb, but it also means fleeting, and being subject to "falling sickness," that is, being susceptible to epilepsy. Epilepsy is classically known as the disease of prophecy, contracted by those who would be seers. A "cad" holds as its primary meaning that of being "a familiar spirit," even as its most contemporary meaning is that of an ungentlemanly betrayer of the affection of women. The word "cadaver" suggests a body from which the spirit has flown. "Cad" is closely associated with the word "cadet," which means "youngest son." "Cadre," the framework for the organization of a troop regiment, is also associated with "cad." So there is something about the caducous character of the loss of Waldo that turns Emerson to thinking about spirit, not simply the lost spirit of his son, but the loss of spirit that is constitutive of our failure to experience fully our lives. We cannot experience without spirit: this insight is one of Emerson's lessons to Nietzsche. The invocation of loss for Emerson must be an incantation of spirit, like a prayer, or it is no invocation at all, simply a howling in the night, timeless, spaceless, desolate.

Emerson turns toward the West, not to fulfill a utopian vision, but to conjure a spiritual return of the dead. This is what it means to thrive by casualties. Against Emerson's idea that there is a realm of thought on a higher plane than the world of experience, or more flatly, against the notion that a neo-Platonic realm of mental self-reliance renders all attempts to act upon the world a necessary corruption of the highest form of self-reliance, this conjuring of spirit can be thought of as a way of diminishing our ever-present lack of presence, our never-to-be-completely-overcome temporal and spatial isolations. This conjuring is what might be called the Emersonian event. In the concluding passages of "Experience," Emerson gestures toward the means through which we might act upon the world, not through "manipular attempts to realize the world of thought" but through a realization that the influence of what we are to know about the world remains open to us as a question. Because it is an open question, the means of moving to address or front it is a practice of patience: "Patience and patience, we shall win at the last." This patience is necessary if we are to live our skepticism, and not deny or repress it. But what are we to win? "And the true romance which the world exists to realize, will be the transformation of genius into practical power" (492).

For some, practical power is utility, and would seem to be the obvious end of a useful political ideology. For those attracted to that kind of relevance, the goal may be to turn losers into winners, and to do so without the need to invoke the memory of loss. But while such an ideology would try to forget or suppress loss, repeating the trauma that Butler notes as a condition of our post-9/11 politics, it could not hope to memorialize loss, because for the utilitarian this kind of memorializing could only be understood as sinking into a morass of regret. Such a forgetfulness is not the practical power that Emerson would have us invoke. A theory of action is required, but this theory would not begin by turning the idea of power into a utility.

But neither would such a theory limit action to the confines of a realm called "the political." Such attempts to constrain action might be comprehended as examples of what Emerson referred to as the clutching at objects that lets them slip through our fingers, the evanescence and lubricity of those objects being "the most unhandsome part of our condition" (473).[15] We are better off when we understand our unhandsome condition in its fullness, when we acknowledge the insight that directness and clarity are not the most valuable of values when it comes to the actions that matter the most to us. We might better realize that, in Emerson's terms, "Our relations with each other are oblique and casual" (473). Again, we may see the double edge—our chief experiences are casual, our relations with each other are casual, our death-bound selves are living amongst our causalities, we thrive by casualties.

"Thinking is a partial act," Emerson writes in "The American Scholar." Living is the total act.[16] Living is beyond capture by our direction; living is a fecundity that we cannot claim for any partial purpose, no matter how important that purpose may be. It is with this turn in his thought that Emerson moves from transcendence to immanence, from the untouchable to the embrace of corporeal life. To acknowledge the partial nature of action in this way is to come to terms with the futility of total thought, and to turn from the absolute isolation of untouchability to the partial actions that are indefinitely available to us in an open field of life. This formulation helps us to dissolve the tendentious distinction that we commonly make between mind and body, and allows us to acknowledge, as Emerson does in his essay on the poet, that "words are also actions, and actions are a kind of words."[17]

Our words are actions, and our actions are words that we put into play in order to realize the world. And yet the world is an intractable and unjust place. If the invocation of loss performs the work of mourning and allows us some means to advance through the world by acts of transformation, we will be on our way to reinspiriting the world. Emerson's cheering words at the end of "Experience," "Never mind the ridicule, never mind the defeat: up again, old heart!" (492) are as hard-earned as any words in our lexicon. The heart turns, overcomes its losses, and moves forward. It does so through the resources of our words, our words which are actions, through the tropes (turns) that mark and record, re-member us, in the common wealth of language and experience.

In and through democracy the possibility of returning is a mode of invoking that may be indefinitely available to anyone who takes steps. Thus it is that mourning is tied to the public sphere. In a time when democracy is in recession, what resources are available to take such steps, and for whom? Democratic claimants of Emerson's inheritance might be able to take heart by observing the reckoning of loss undertaken by W. E. B. Du Bois.

Unhopeful Hope

As Emerson grieved the loss of his son Waldo, so too did Du Bois grieve the loss of his son Burghardt. Du Bois's reflection on the death of his son takes up only a few pages of *The Souls of Black Folk*.

But it serves as a response to and even a deepening of Emerson's working through the condition of grief. Du Bois's grief appears to contrast strongly with Emerson's, and initially this seems to depend extravagantly, if silently, on the privileges Emerson enjoyed as a free white male New England property owner, as someone who could look forward to the abolition of slavery as the achievement of justice, as someone who, while feeling the pain of the slave as a silencing of the processes by which we all might be free, nonetheless was privileged to observe all of this from the comfort of his home in Concord, Massachusetts. Du Bois, also a Harvard graduate and a leading intellectual of his age, did not enjoy the privileges of Emerson, and this was only because he was a Negro, a colored person. So if we are to acknowledge his loss, we must try to reckon into the calculus of loss this horrible stain of injustice as a part of the experience of Du Bois, and perhaps not of Emerson. And as democrats, we must try to reckon not only his loss, but his loss as multiplied by the millions of others who one by one have suffered it directly, as its most prominent victims; indirectly, as witnesses who have so far been muted in response to the damage it has done to us; and partially, as our collective inheritance of a culture. This loss must become something else than it is if we are to turn our losses into gains. If we hope to take steps in Du Bois's experience of grief, our first step is to acknowledge how all of us are stained.

Another way of putting this is to suggest that Du Bois's reflection on the death of his son is informed by the double-consciousness that racism imposes as a life condition for those subject to its regime—which means all of us who think we have inherited something from the culture of the United States—as we look backward to the moment of freedom from a life of *de jure* segregation. Then we might ask, how does this racism make a difference for the experience of grief? For Du Bois, grief is inscribed in the life of the child who is mourned:

Within the Veil was he born, said I; and there shall he live,—a
Negro and a Negro's son. Holding in that little head—ah,
bitterly!—the unbowed pride of a hunted race, clinging with
that tiny dimpled hand—ah, wearily!—to a hope not hopeless
but unhopeful, and seeing with those bright wondering eyes
that peer into my soul a land whose freedom is to us a mockery
and whose liberty is a lie, I saw the shadow of the Veil as it
passed over my baby, I saw the cold city towering above the
blood-red land.[18]

Du Bois grieves his son upon the occasion of his son's birth! He sees
something like the inversion of a redemption narrative taking place
here. The echoes of the experience of Moses and of the Exodus narrative are clear, if complicated. A shadow passes over this baby; the
Veil condemns this first-born child to a life like death. A flight is in
the offing, but where are the people to go?

The influence of Emerson is also clear. "A hope not hopeless but
unhopeful" echoes "I grieve that grief can teach me nothing." The
clinging hand is the unhandsome condition of the seeker of certain
truth. An unhopeful hope is what Du Bois has to offer his first-
born son as the legacy of the wise father. "I too mused above his
little white bed; saw the strength of my own arm stretched onward
through the ages through the newer strength of his; saw the dream
of my black fathers stagger a step onward in the wild phantasm of
the world; heard in his baby voice the voice of the Prophet that was
to rise within the Veil" (160).

The step that Du Bois imagines is transposed across generations.
If Emerson wants us to try to intensify our presence in the present,
Du Bois asks us to imagine the alternative futures that might emerge
as inheritances of the past, to imagine what the opening to the future might hold for those who seek to escape the confinement of a
present built upon a sordid past. His historical sense socializes the

journey of recovery in a manner that complements but extends the Emersonian imagination of the social as the return to us of our rejected thoughts with an alienated majesty. The depth of alienation becomes tragic, the majesty quasi-religious, yet still bound to history. Du Bois's step is a staggering one, but a step nonetheless, into a new world, a rebirth. For Du Bois, this new yet unapproachable America becomes the wild phantasm of the world. The Emersonian practice of patience is stretched, extended from one generation to the next, as the everyday is preserved within the hardship of the smallest movement forward. And the modesty of Emerson—"I know better than to claim any completeness for my picture. I am a fragment, and this is a fragment of me" (491)—is stretched as well, in Du Bois's notice of the hard indifference of death as life goes on all around it. In describing the moment of Burghardt's death, he writes: "The day changed not; the same tall trees peeped in at the windows, the same green grass glinted in the setting sun" (161). Against this tragedy there is the duration of the day, indifferent, a sky, the same sky, everywhere he goes.

The days of Du Bois are not the same as the days of Emerson. How could they be? The difference between them is inscribed in the divisions that constitute the shadow of the Veil. The color-line, which had not yet harmed the boy in his young life—"in his little world walked souls alone, uncolored and unclothed"—caught up to him after death, a moment too late to hurt him, but ever decisive for his wise father. As the first-born's family proceeded through the streets of Atlanta to lay him to rest, they heard the pale-faced men and women utter the word that measures the distance from one side of the Veil to the other, an indefinitely open, infinitely deep divide: "Niggers!"

> We could not lay him in the ground there in Georgia, for the earth there is strangely red; so we bore him away to the north-

ward, with his flowers and his little folded hands. In vain, in vain!—for where, O God! Beneath thy broad blue sky shall my dark baby rest in peace,—where Reverence dwells, and Goodness, and a Freedom that is free? (162)

A word is an action, and an action is a word. A word propelled the family to the north to bury young Burghardt, but Du Bois is not so foolish as to think he will find relief there: there is no freedom that is free. No place to rest. Again, we must account for this difference, and in doing so take upon ourselves the stain of racism as our debt, and hope that it will enable us to acknowledge the indefinitely deep grief of Du Bois. A latter-day Antigone, Du Bois renews the claim that she makes for other forms of kinship, for the right to die—and hence, live—in dignity.

Where does this compounded grief leave Du Bois? Where does he find himself? Does he have anywhere to turn? The final paragraph of his chapter, in its conventional expressions of a parent's wish ("If one must have gone, why not I?") seems far from the invocation that Emerson makes on behalf of his Waldo, but its final note of encouragement echoes Emerson. It suggests a metaphor for comparing two equations of America.

The wretched of my race that line the alleys of the nation sit fatherless and unmothered; but Love sat beside his cradle, and in his ear Wisdom waited to speak. Perhaps now he knows the All-love, and needs not to be wise. Sleep, then, child,—sleep til I sleep and waken to a baby voice and the ceaseless patter of little feet—above the Veil. (163)

Du Bois is Wisdom, his wife is Love, and their son in his death knows All-love and has no need to be wise. Whose baby voice, whose little feet will patter above the Veil? Will Du Bois himself in death be stripped of wisdom, and hopefully born again, will he clap his hands in infantine joy at this America that does not yet exist for him except in visions of an after-death?

"Nothing is left us now but death. We look to that with a grim satisfaction, saying, there at least is reality that will not dodge us," writes Emerson in his essay on grief (473). What is this after-death for which we are to be prepared to die? For Du Bois it is the way to be above the Veil, the pain of a deeply invidious distinction. For Emerson, it is the finitude that grounds the indefinitely open approach to the possibility that we might attain some measure of hope in our hopeless situation. Both of them call it God. For those of us who think that the evocation of God is but one way to refer to the enchantment of the world, their common hope prepares us for a true romance.

For Emerson, the reality that will not escape us, the predictable ordinary of temperament, that lord of life, is also death, the determination of our fate, with one exception. "In every intelligence there is a door through which the creator passes" (475). This is the passage of spirit, the moment of return, the spiritual being, that which is its own evidence. The passage of spirit might allow us to die out of Nature and be born again. And so too for Du Bois, who sees in the Sorrow Songs the gifts of story and song, of sweat and brawn, and of Spirit. He asks, "Would America have been America without her Negro people?" (193). Du Bois will be born again with a baby voice, will come into his own as an American, when the possibility of the Afterthought becomes, again like a prayer, born in the wilderness, ever becoming.

> *Hear my cry, O God the Reader, vouchsafe that this my book fall not still-born into the world-wilderness . . . Thus in Thy good time may infinite reason turn the tangle straight, and these crooked marks on a fragile leaf be not indeed*
> THE END (195)

This is Du Bois's prayer, that the end not be The End, that a stumble-step forward be his legacy, to Burghardt and to us. He ends this chapter of *The Souls of Black Folk* without a final period, a final stop, encouraging more marks, a movement forward.

(Re)Turning to Politics

We are the readers, the gods for whom these words are written, and every day we turn a new leaf. The leaves of Walden, the leaves of grass, the vinelands of California, the hemp that forms the ropes on which strange fruit is hung as Du Bois composes his book and life. The possibility of being free in a new America not yet approachable, to be born again, not still-born but facing the endless writing of ourselves, turning our tropes into troops, our cadets into cads, allowing the grief to fall away, and the spirit to come in—this is the hardest work we can do. This is a practical power that we realize in the discourses of freedom available to us as a specific inheritance of American political thought. It will perhaps someday make it not matter to be American, which is also the best that we can possibly hope for.

The losses that Emerson and Du Bois sustained are profoundly ordinary. Whatever sense we might gain from the record of their struggles—from the crooked marks on fragile leaves—we can acknowledge that they more or less sustained the capacity to see the worst and offer more than that for our consideration. If we are to understand them as references, as guides, we need to try to think an amazingly shocking thought: that even now, even after Auschwitz, even after Hiroshima, even after Stalinism, even after Tiananmen Square, even after bleeding Africa, even after the mushrooming carceral, starving children, dispossessed families, cynical capital, preemptive war, American torturers, Darfur, Palestine, on and on, even after every conflagration we might take note of that stands as an unanswered accusation that the twentieth century has been the bloodiest in history, with a twenty-first threatening to be worse, even after we succeed in connecting this bloodiness to Du Bois's prophecy concerning the color line, the worst is still not that bad, at least not yet. "This time, like all times, is a very good one, if we but know what to do with it," is what Emerson writes in the face of slavery, in anticipation of or prophecy of civil war.[19]

When we turn back to the world from the place of loss, we might come to know that turning, not necessarily as redemptive, but as resignative, as a re-signing of our contract to be with others. Thus the turn toward the world from a place of loss is the turn toward politics, toward constructing common and uncommon spaces of agonistic exchange and misunderstanding, of revelation and projection, of new coinages and destructions, partial and fragmentary, neither utopian nor dystopian, but, as Emerson would suggest, encompassing both. For those purposes, we engage in politics not only when we act together, but when we act apart. The injustices we struggle to ameliorate and rectify, the capacity for connection and openness we seek to cultivate, the pleasures we might take in the variety of adventures in becoming—adventures that are indefinitely available to anyone and everyone, and that we might intuit as our democratic inheritance—are the constitutive elements of political gesture and conspiracy. When we conspire, we breathe together, we inspirit each other, and so our selves. In doing so, we do not overcome the lonely self. Instead, we infuse affirmation and connection into the lonely self without departing from it. We acknowledge our need to take on our loneliness as a measure of our selves.

The attendance to the everyday is, I think, the point of the matter, the endless end of democratic life. And to the extent that one crisis or another—what Walter Benjamin once called the permanent state of emergency[20]—compels us to turn away from the everyday and toward epochal pretensions, democratic life is imperiled as much by the distracted attention we pay to the conditions of emergency as it is to the fact of emergency itself. We might think of the terms of our bewilderment in ways that allow us to escape, if only temporarily, the integrative willfulness of the epochal thinker. For while our bewilderment is partly a consequence of the numbness many democrats have experienced in response to the unrelentingly hostile and often duplicitous attacks on democratic thinking by reactionaries, it is also a result of what we might call a loss of metaphorical purchase. This loss is registered not as a failure of thinking itself but as a manifestation of the "danger" that Martin Heidegger identified in his meditation on technology, as a way our thinking is continuously being reduced to a relentless positivity.

In 1966 Thomas Pynchon described in compelling terms the eerie sensibility underlying such a loss of metaphorical purchase. In his novel *The Crying of Lot 49*, the heroine, Oedipa Maas, discusses entropy with John Nefastis, a man who has a Machine that he claims can do the work of Maxwell's Demon, gathering information while losing entropy, all because the equations for the loss of energy and the loss of information look alike.

> "Entropy is a figure of speech, then," sighed Nefastis, "a metaphor. It connects the world of thermodynamics to the world of information flow. The Machine uses both. The Demon makes the metaphor not only verbally graceful, but also objectively true."
>
> "But what," she felt like some kind of a heretic, "if the Demon exists only because the two equations look alike? Because of the metaphor?"
>
> Nefastis smiled; impenetrable, calm, a believer. "He existed for Clark Maxwell long before the days of the metaphor."[21]

Those things that exist *for* us—before the relevant metaphor comes into being through parallel yet disconnected experiences—are not yet available *to* us, and when they become available *to* us—after metaphor—they cease to be available *for* us. This paradox makes the task of active thinking perilous. It brings us to the brink of ceasing to be, to the end of our existential possibilities. We may find ourselves lost between past and future, and unable to acknowledge the extent to which our present is thus diminished. And yet this is the tension we must sustain if we are to be true to our ghosts, to the haunting of our lives by those whom we love and fear.

The fact of the death of a loved one for those of us who are left behind runs in an inverted parallel to the entropic metaphor of Maxwell's Demon. Death is an objective fact, the fact of final disappearance. My wife, as a thing, no longer exists, and hence is never again to be available *for* me, but through the fact of her irretrievable absence she is insistently, still sometimes overwhelmingly, available *to* me. Grief gives her a profound presence in my ongoing life; her ghost, even in its exhausted state, comforts me and frightens me. This is how she is real to me. In my long nights she is silent, I cry to her, I follow her though bizarre dreamscapes, and allow myself to miss her. As her presence as absence comes to be integrated into my life, I begin to lose her again; in her real absence she becomes a metaphor for my real loss of her—she becomes, as Emerson says, a part of my estate. In this way she is caducous, sloughed off of me, put irretrievably into my memory, as a fixed and separate piece of my very personal past. There will be moments of life in that memory, but not as vivid as my childhood memories, strangely.

I will always remember the memory of her.

Is this too harsh an assessment? Could it be that I am simply a cold and calculating man, living off the estate of my dead wife? I hope not; I don't think so, regardless of my many flaws; but how am I to know who I am if I fail to make this turn away from her and back to the world? If I do not finish, however incompletely, my grieving for her, what am I to do? On the other hand, I will never finish this grieving, and it would be foolish not to realize the gift this casualty has been for me. In the loss of my wife, I gained a world. To deny that is to deny her presence in my life, her presence as a ghost, the integrity of which I must honor.

If these questions apply to me, they must also apply to all who are grieving. In a time of cynical war and refused grief among those who are leading this country, it is possible to distinguish between those of us who are grieving well and those who are not on the basis of Butler's criterion—those who refuse to grieve fully are engaging in politically devastating action. A president who hides the coffins, who refuses to go to funerals for the dead, who celebrates the death of his proclaimed enemies with relish and vigor, who encourages us to consume and refuses to lead us to honest sacrifice, who escalates simply to avoid his personal embarrassment when it is clear that the war is lost, is pursuing a politics of blocked grief. In his isolation, his sovereign madness, his stupidity, he is leading a nation to a place where our citizenry is unable to move forward, unable to go back, unable to reenter history, unable to do anything other than lash out at those who would have us begin the process of sloughing off our loss. This is the trauma we are faced with—political leaders who are unwilling or unable to be losers, grievers. This may in fact be the deepest danger we are presented with as the new millennium unfolds, that our leaders are still unwilling and unable to think about themselves as human beings, but instead believe they must be self-contained isolatoes, our most representative lonely persons.

Yet there are signs of life all around us. As we become more aware of this harm, we are presented with the terms of our always possible conversion. Our incredibly shrinking past and future might help us understand the work of thought as the work of trying to convert despair into hope, because this always partial and incomplete process, while entailing the remembrance of the loss of metaphorical certainty, also involves the finding (founding) of a will to live through the skepticism that a loss of certainty about past and future itself entails. If this turn toward living through skepticism were unavailable to us, the wisdom of Silenus—that it would have been best never to have lived at all—would surely prevail. Living through our skepticism (the overcoming of entropy), as Pynchon noticed, takes the form of a demonic hope we might hold as thinkers—for thinking is our action—to work through the powers of skepticism, not to emerge into a new Kingdom of God, but to try again, and fail again, and try harder, to borrow from Samuel Beckett.

Fail again. The word "lose" expresses the experience of devastation, ruin, misery, but it is also noted as being a term of praise, renown, and fame. "Loss" expresses dissolution—with all of its ambiguities, since dissolution and solution, dissolving and solving, etymologically mean the same thing—but it also in its archaic sense expresses the breaking up of the ranks of an army. Out of a sense of loss we might be tempted to break up the army of thought, to dissolve the cadres of thinking. But our army of tropes and metaphors might be redeployed instead. We redeploy our tropes (we support our troops) in our various attempts to recover from our losses, when we return to the scene of the crime of consent, when we give the lie to our failure in the very enunciation of it.[22] Try again.

Try again, fail again, try harder. What could be a better motto for those who grieve, for those of us who have experienced the loss of our loved ones, whether it be through death or death's many surrogates? In our struggles we may realize something else as well, that our loneliest moments may be behind us.

Epilogue

Writing

Despair and a sense of loss are not static conditions, but goads to our labors.

—Stanley Cavell

In June of 2005 my older brother persuaded me to meet him in Africa, where he was visiting the national offices and other operations in Ethiopia and Kenya for the non-governmental organization he directed. I had just completed my teaching for the academic year and was at the beginning of a year-long sabbatical. I still was grieving the loss of my wife almost two years earlier, and I know my brother thought that the trip might be a good way to distract me, to jar me out of my melancholy. I too thought such a journey could be a good way to get away from myself.

I am not a particularly well-traveled person, having only recently been to Europe for the first time, and once traveling to Australia, in both cases to attend academic conferences. This trip was different. The route to Africa—from Boston to Amsterdam, through Khartoum, ultimately landing in Addis Ababa late on a Saturday night—was thrilling. My sense of worldliness was intensified by a strange coincidence. One of the vice presidents of the University of Addis Ababa was a political philosopher who had taught some years ago at Williams College, and happened to be an old acquaintance of mine. My brother had his Ethiopian representative contact him, and arrangements were made for me to lecture at the university on Monday morning. I was to discuss the political climate of the United States following the events of 9/11.

On Sunday, still jet-lagged, I accompanied my brother and his country representative to the Ethiopian National Museum. While there, we went down to a basement room where we viewed the bones of Lucy, the oldest found remains of a humanoid on the face of the earth. Later that day we visited the former palace of Haile Selassie, the last emperor of Ethiopia (which had been converted into a museum and the administrative offices of the university), getting a tour of his private quarters. I also heard from my host at the university that my lecture had been canceled. He explained that there wasn't a large enough audience, that the university was on break. He invited me instead to meet on Monday morning with him and the president of the university.

The meeting never took place. Sunday evening I turned on the television in my hotel room and learned that the students who were supposedly on break were actually going on strike to protest the national government's withholding of the results of the spring election, which, rumor had it, had resulted in a defeat for the incumbent prime minister's government. The army came onto the university grounds that evening and arrested hundreds of students. Early Monday morning, my old acquaintance called my hotel room. He explained to me that the university was closed, that the students were "acting up." He assured me that we would be able to meet later in the week, that this was simply a minor matter involving a few disgruntled opposition politicians, fomenting unrest among the student population.

But Monday night army troops fired into a crowd of protesters, and close to two hundred were killed. Tuesday the cab drivers of Addis Ababa went on strike, and later that day martial law was declared. My brother and I left the city the next morning, flying in turn to Aksum, a small and ancient city near the contested border with Eritrea, and then to Gondor, the medieval capital of Ethiopia, at the source of the Blue Nile. As we traveled through the countryside, meeting health workers, visiting rural families in their homes, far from the capital city, we learned more about the crackdown and heard of arrests being made throughout the country. We returned to Addis Ababa at the end of the week to a transformed political landscape.

I left Ethiopia without ever meeting with the former professor from Williams. I did speak to him on the telephone one last time, conveying greetings from old friends in the United States, expressing my concern over the violence and my worry for himself and his family's personal safety. He laughingly assured me that this would all blow over shortly. But it didn't. In the ensuing weeks and months, the more I learned about what had happened that week, the sadder I felt. The massacre that occurred that June is now referred to as Ethiopia's Tiananmen Square. The country is now a much harsher place than it was when we first visited; its army, the largest in Africa, is fighting as a proxy for the Bush administration against Somalia, threatening war with Eritrea, fighting against rebels in the southeastern region of the country, with many opposition politicians in prison and still no free elections. And my old acquaintance has since risen to the highest levels of the Ethiopian government.

I had imagined before I left for Africa that something would happen to me as a consequence of that trip. I thought that somehow there would be an enlargement of my life, that the experience would change me. And the trip was, in retrospect, amazing. Surely, if only for the sake of tropes, as Thoreau might put it, visiting the mythical palace grounds of the Queen of Sheba, walking around the outside of the Coptic church guarded by a single monk day and night, where according to legend the Ark of the Covenant was entombed, gazing upon the obelisks of Aksum, walking through the bedroom of the last emperor in the palace in Addis Ababa, an emperor whose lineage supposedly dated back to Solomon, roaming through the countryside of one of the most ancient nations on the face of the earth, being present during a period of tragic political turmoil—surely these experiences would provoke something in me.

But when I came home, my wife was still gone, my children still needed me, and the basic conditions of my existence remained pretty much the same.

Nonetheless, there was one change, a change that mattered then and still does. Upon my return home, after years of preparations and false starts, I began writing this book. It has become clear to me that the return to my writing has been the occasion of whatever change there has been in me. After my wife was diagnosed with cancer but before she died, a good friend suggested that I might not be able to write by drawing upon personal experience anymore, that this sort of suffering is not available for the kind of writing that focuses on the politics of the ordinary, that such a discussion, such a form of critical thinking, is not appropriate to such a subject. For the longest time I thought she might be right, that the available common storehouse of language simply would not make it possible for me to get to that place. But something happened along the way. My attempt to write became a point of the writing, a way for me to reach a better sense of loneliness as a way of life. I learned in my heart something that my head had been tutored in for years, but that I had not yet fully comprehended—that it is through this process of discovery, available to us through the use of our language, that it becomes possible to imagine a way forward, toward a continuous becoming, another turn.

Those thinkers who have mattered the most to me have always kept the possibility of change, a kind of transformation or conversion through the conversation of their words, open to us. Every one of them has proceeded in his or her own way, acutely aware of his or her own limits, but also of the possibility, always present, of being outstripped by their own selves. And yet none of them has been where I have been, or is going where I am going, except for our final destinations. My companions—and you readers, it turns out, are among them to varying degrees—can confidently claim this station as another step on our common road to nowhere, and we write and read to tell each other how we are to be lonely together.

So much of our way forward has to do with the reading and writing of words. Why this is so requires some explanation. In his chapter on "Sounds" in *Walden*, Thoreau writes, "Much is published, but little printed."[1] Commenting on the importance of words themselves for Thoreau, Stanley Cavell suggests that "the remark . . . describes the ontological condition of words; the occurrence of a word is the occurrence of an object whose placement always has a point, and whose point always lies before and beyond it. 'The volatile truth of our words should continually betray the inadequacy of the residual statement. Their truth is instantly translated; its literal monument alone remains'" (563).[2] The placement of a word in a sentence is the representation of the presence of the present in writing. It is itself a way of compressing time—so it is no accident that Thoreau compresses two years into one in his writing, or that he astonishingly says toward the end of *Walden*, "Thus was my first year's life in the woods completed; and the second was similar to it" (558).

But the intense economy of such a kind of writing does more than compress time. Thoreau's politics of becoming is most intensely expressed through his commitment to his writing as a way of being in the world. How is that so? Cavell suggests the following:

> In *Walden*, reading is not merely the other side of writing, its eventual fate; it is another metaphor of writing itself. The writer

cannot invent words as "perpetual suggestions and provoca-
tions" [353]; the written word is already "the choicest of relics"
[355]. His calling depends upon his acceptance of this fact about
words, his letting them come to him from their own region,
and then taking that occasion for inflecting them one way instead of another then and there; as one may inflect the earth
toward beans instead of grass, or let it alone, as it is before you
are there. (28)

In other words, the work of the writer, when raised to the appropriate level of awareness of words, becomes a way of doing the work of
becoming. Under the right conditions we cultivate in ourselves a
receptivity, an awareness of the linkage of words to sentences, of the
multiple registers with which we may receive and transmit meaning
through the vehicle of our writing. For it is also the case that writing is a labor of the hands. "Writing, at its best, will come to a finish in each mark of meaning, in each portion and sentence and
word. That is why in reading it 'we must laboriously seek the meaning of every word and line; conjecturing a larger sense' [353]"
(Cavell, 27–28).

If the labor of writing is to be the other side of reading, then it
behooves us to think further about our reading as a conjecture, to
imagine what it means to be present as a reader as well as a writer in
this larger sense. To conjecture is to reach a judgment on the basis
of inconclusive or incomplete information. All of us live lives of
conjecture, practically balancing our acts, operating inconclusively,
improvising on the basis of partial evidence. This is how we become
who we are. You may imagine this book to be filled with conjecture, a striving toward a larger sense of who I am becoming than I
had when I began. As all writers do, I have engaged in the laborious
process of representing my thoughts, projecting them for the conjecture of my readers, conjecturing myself as I translate my thought/
feelings into words, reading what I write, and then rewriting. All

writing, in this sense, is rewriting. The labor of writing is most fully realized when it approaches the level of deliberateness that Thoreau's conjectural leap demands.

To express our selves in this way is to try to illuminate the conditions of possibility for the writing of an essay, an attempt to say something about our selves to our selves and to each other about our provisional existence. Those conditions, it turns out, are synonymous with the conditions of our thinking, our living, our confronting and engaging our lives. Thoreau understood that writing was the vehicle for such an engagement, his way of being present in his present. He expressed this when he wrote, "In any weather, at any hour of day or night, I have been anxious to improve upon the nick of time, and notch it on my stick too; to stand on the meeting of two eternities, the past and the future, which is precisely the present moment; to toe that line" (272). For him, to notch time upon his stick is to write through the experience of being present. Such a writing is also a practice of thinking, a way of recovering ourselves, what Cavell has suggested is Thoreau's commitment to having his writing and his life manifest each other (9). It is what we may call a way of being sane with ourselves, living in the acknowledgment of a great absence, without prospect of anything beyond the duration of time, aware of our marking of it, writing it, looking closely at the conditions of our own possibility, of our sanity in the writing of our lives, alone together.

I will someday return to Ethiopia, and think again about what happened (and didn't) while I was there. Perhaps I will be able to write about my new experiences. But I hope, before I go there again, that I will have better considered this piece of advice from Thoreau concerning travel:

> One hastens to Southern Africa to chase the giraffe; but surely that is not the game he would be after. How long, pray, would a man hunt giraffes if he could? Snipes and woodcocks also afford

rare sport; but I trust it would be nobler game to shoot one's
self.

> "Direct your eye right inward, and you'll find
> A thousand regions in your mind
> Yet undiscovered. Travel them, and be
> Expert in home-cosmography."

What does Africa, what does the West, stand for? Is not our
own interior white on the chart? black though it may prove,
like the coast, when discovered. Is it the source of the Nile, or
the Niger, or the Mississippi, or a Northwest Passage around
this continent, that we would find? . . . If you would learn to
speak all tongues and conform to all the customs of all nations,
if you would travel farther than all travelers, be naturalized in
all climes, and cause the Sphinx to dash her head against a
stone, even obey the precept of the old philosopher, and Explore thyself. (559–561)

Thoreau was cautionary about travel, not because he thought travel
useless, but because he worried about it as a distraction from the
greater and more important exploration, to the sources of our
selves, those bottomless ponds that have a bottom after all. Our
home-cosmography—this writing of our universal dwelling—has
as much to tell us about what is essential to ourselves as any other
thing we may discover in the wider world.

Our exploration is endless, until in due course we come to an
end, and for us moderns the exploration advances in the face of the
great loneliness that has been our inheritance. Our loneliness is always deepest in those moments when we face the terror of nothing.
But nothing rarely appears as itself; instead, it takes on many guises,
most of which connect back to the ultimate nothing, death, or non-
existence, that blank page. We embrace loneliness as a solace from
that pain. But there is an everlasting price we pay for this embrace.
Our sorrow, our pain, our community of nothing in common re-

cedes from view, and we become ghostly in our existence. We come to haunt ourselves, rather than explore ourselves. This is what was worst for Thoreau—to witness so many ghostly people, chained to possessions, striving to escape themselves, unable to see that earlier dawn.

What are we to do with our selves in the face of our losses? I have written this book in the face of all sorts of ordinary losses. Some of them have been dramatic, but even the small ones are tinged with a sadness that echoes beyond immediate circumstance. The most recent is the departure of my only daughter from home, leaving me and her younger brother on our own, ill prepared to negotiate our way through our everyday existence with each other. We'll manage without her, but I will be thinking about what it means to embrace a life in which children leave home in order to be in the world. Of course, the family that sheltered Irene is also the inevitable source of her traumas. Her strengths, her weaknesses, are woven together into the very fabric of her existence. Perhaps she will learn something from reading this book, something I otherwise could not give her, my motherless daughter—my only words of advice, to perdure in front of the fact of her loneliness, stubborn, resilient, sorrowful, yes, but smiling, gentle, listening, meeting the infinite with patient finitude, flapping her wings, being still as a pond, peering into the eyes of others as though she is the first ever to see.

The lonely self will always be with us now, an elemental part of our human being. It is a fact too late to be helped. Yet as long as we continue to exist, we may also come to realize that as alone as we are, we are not only alone. Being aware of our paths to conversion, to the changes we may make in the writing of our lives together and apart, to the aversion of what so many of us *call* conversion, cheers me and encourages me, even in the face of our common catastrophe. That we do not know our next step does not mean that we are lost. It only means that we have yet to find ourselves.

Notes

Prologue

1. All citations of *The Tragedy of King Lear* by William Shakespeare are from *The Riverside Shakespeare* (Boston: Houghton Mifflin, 1974).

2. *The Compact Edition of the Oxford English Dictionary* (New York: Oxford University Press, 1991), definition III.12.a.

3. Stanley Cavell, *Must We Mean What We Say? A Book of Essays*, chap. X, "The Avoidance of Love: A Reading of *King Lear*" (Cambridge: Cambridge University Press, 1976; originally published by Charles Scribner's Sons, 1969), 289. Subsequent references are identified by page numbers in the text.

4. When we attempt to think about Cordelia's inheritance to us, it is relevant to remember as well that Cavell's occasion for thinking about Lear and his daughter was a national tragedy, ongoing, of a nation that at its best does not exist as a nation, a polity born of a revolution that was not a civil war, a country that fought a civil war that was not a revolution, a country that knows little of its power and fears only its impotence. At the time of the writing of "The Avoidance of Love" in the late 1960s, soldiers from this country were destroying villages in order to save them, troops were killing young people to try to prove that the country could continue to live with itself. Thirty-odd years later, at the time of this writing, the dissolution of what is strangely called a bipolar world has given way to shades of ruined empire, and at the empty heart of globalization, struggling with its absent presence as the first metapower, is the network power called the United States of America. Again we are destroying in order to save; again we are divided.

I. Being

1. From David Riesman and his colleagues' *The Lonely Crowd*, to Philip Slater's *The Pursuit of Loneliness*, to Christopher Lasch's related studies, *Haven in a Heartless World* and *The Culture of Narcissism*, through the

survey of American attitudes presented in Robert Bellah and his colleagues' study *Habits of the Heart,* and reaching a certain apotheosis in Robert Putnam's *Bowling Alone* (a neo-Tocquevillian cry from the heart disguised as a work of survey research), there emerges a constant and powerful claim concerning the sorry state of what for better or worse has been termed "the American character."

2. Michel Foucault, *Discipline and Punish: The Birth of the Prison,* trans. Alan Sheridan (New York: Pantheon, 1977), 221.

3. I know that I am hardly the first to be concerned about the politics of loneliness. The topic is so firmly embedded in the recent history of political and social thought as to render a bibliography of the subject virtually useless, since it could easily correspond to the library of that thought itself. Nonetheless, it may be useful to note that some of the most prominent works of the century just passed are concerned with the consequences of loneliness for the life of the polity. The theme may be conceived as the core concern of such diverse yet deeply connected thinkers of the twentieth century as Max Weber, Martin Heidegger, Hannah Arendt, Jean-Paul Sartre, Theodor Adorno, Walter Benjamin, Isaiah Berlin, and Michel Foucault. In our present, other equally diverse thinkers who have struggled to give shape to the themes of contemporary political thought, such as Charles Taylor, Jürgen Habermas, William Connolly, Sheldon Wolin, Judith Butler, George Kateb, Stanley Cavell, and John Rawls, have had to make their specific claims concerning the problems of political life address the powerful affective forces associated with loneliness, especially the twinned phenomena of *ressentiment* and alienation, powerful themes for two extraordinary minds of the nineteenth century, Karl Marx and Friedrich Nietzsche.

4. See Elaine Scarry, *The Body in Pain: The Making and Unmaking of the World* (New York: Oxford University Press, 1985), chap. 1.

5. Emerson, Thoreau, Wittgenstein, Austin, and Cavell suggest this from one tradition, while Foucault, Deleuze, Butler, and Connolly suggest it from another, not unrelated, tradition.

6. For a recent summary statement of his philosophical argument concerning this relationship, see Stanley Cavell, *Cities of Words* (Cambridge, Mass.: Harvard University Press, 2004). Thoreau's statements concerning resignation can be found in *Walden.* For my understanding of resignation, see Thomas L. Dumm, "Resignation," *Critical Inquiry,* vol. 25, no. 1 (Fall 1998), 56–76.

7. Hannah Arendt, *The Origins of Totalitarianism* (New York: Harcourt, Brace, 1952), hereafter cited as OT. Subsequent references are identified by page numbers in the text.

8. Hannah Arendt, "We Refugees," *The Menorah Journal,* vol. 22, no. 3 (1943), 69–77. This essay has recently been reprinted in Hannah Arendt, *The Jewish Writings,* ed. Jerome Kohn and Ron H. Feldman (New York: Shocken Books, 2007), 264–274. All subsequent references in the text by page number are to the Shocken publication.

9. Giorgio Agamben, *Homo Sacer,* trans. Daniel Heller-Roazen (Stanford: Stanford University Press, 1998).

10. Hannah Arendt, *The Human Condition* (Chicago: University of Chicago Press, 1958).

II. Having

1. On the idea of self-ownership generally, and the concept of the behavioral self more specifically, see John Wikse, *About Possession: The Self as Private Property* (University Park: Pennsylvania State University Press, 1977).

2. *Groundhog Day* (directed by Harold Ramis, script by Danny Rubin and Harold Ramis, 1993).

3. Arthur Miller, *Death of a Salesman: Certain Private Conversations in Two Acts and a Requiem,* with an introduction by Christopher Bigsby (New York: Penguin Books, 1998). This remark is quoted in the introduction, citing Robert A. Martin and Steven R. Centola, eds., *The Theatre Essays of Arthur Miller* (New York: Da Capo Press, 1996), 423. The play was first performed at the Morosco Theatre in New York on February 10, 1949. Subsequent references to the play are given in the text as DS, followed by the page number.

4. But other elements may be at work in the shaping of our selves. Judith Butler, for instance, has identified an entire group of what she calls "non-narrativizable" elements of selfhood that contribute to the disappearance of each of our selves into terms that determine us. See Judith Butler, *Giving an Account of Oneself* (New York: Fordham University Press, 2005), 39. Among the elements she mentions are bodily exposure, primary relations with others, a psychic history that is necessarily partial and hence has an opacity to oneself, norms that undermine singularity, and finally a structure of address within which those norms are expressed. All of these work in concert toward the establishment of an account that contributes to making the singular self disappear into itself.

5. Deleuze, quoted by John Rajchman in the introduction to Gilles Deleuze, *Pure Immanence: Essays on a Life,* trans. Ann Boyman (New York: Zone Books, 2001), 18. Subsequent references are identified by page numbers in the text.

6. Eyal Peretz, *Literature, Disaster, and the Enigma of Power: A Reading of Moby-Dick* (Stanford: Stanford University Press, 2003), 36. Subsequent references are identified by page numbers in the text.

7. All direct references to *Moby-Dick* are to specific chapters (C1 is Chapter 1, etc.). I have used the University of California edition of the Arion Press limited edition of 1979 (Berkeley: University of California Press, 1979); this edition is based on the text prepared for Northwestern University Press's critical edition of *Moby-Dick* by Harrison Hayford, Hershel Parker, and G. Thomas Tanselle. I have used this edition as well for its precise illustrations of the whaling ship provided by Barry Moser, which help illustrate the argument I wish to make concerning the identity of Ishmael.

8. My thanks to Tess Taylor for sharing with me her insights into the history of the Randolph family, and in particular for pointing out this important passage.

9. Henry David Thoreau, *Walden,* in *Thoreau* (New York: Library of America, 1985), 328.

III. Loving

1. Henry David Thoreau, *Walden,* chap. 3, "Reading," in *The Portable Thoreau,* ed. Carl Bode (New York: Penguin Books, 1947), 354. All subsequent page references are given in the text.

2. John Locke, *Second Treatise of Government,* ed. C. B. Macpherson (Hackett Publishing Company, 1980; originally published, 1690), VI, "Of Paternal Power," 31.

3. For all the claims we might make concerning the role of the family in modern life as a shaper of the self, as the incubator of citizens, those who have written of the modern family in clinical terms seem largely unaware, or at least unreflective, about the family as a space of deep loneliness. Those who have thought through the role of the family in society in a careful way, such as Christopher Lasch, have too often been harsh in their judgments of those who have struggled to understand the circumstances that have given rise to their despair. The charge of narcissism, which begins as a clinical diagnosis and ends as a moral accusation, is particularly insidious in its effect on those individuals whose journey to self-discovery has entailed grappling with difficult issues of sexual identity and social status. To put it bluntly, to be gay is not to be a narcissist, although this seems to be the upshot of Lasch's work. See Christopher Lasch, *Haven in a Heartless World: The Family Besieged* (New York: Basic Books, 1977), and *The Culture of Narcissism* (New York: Basic Books, 1979).

4. Michel Foucault, *The History of Sexuality*, Volume 1, *An Introduction*, trans. Robert Hurley (New York: Pantheon, 1978), 46.

5. *Paris, Texas* (directed by Wim Wenders, written by Sam Shepard, adaptation by L. M. Kit Carson, 1984, Road Movies Film Produktion, GmbH, DVD 2004, Twentieth Century Fox Home Entertainment). Quotations from the film in this section were transcribed from the DVD.

6. Anne Carson, *Eros the Bittersweet* (Normal, Ill.: Dalkey Archive Press, 1998; originally published by Princeton University Press, 1986), 30.

7. Walter Benjamin, *A Berlin Childhood* (Cambridge, Mass.: Harvard University Press, 2006).

IV. Grieving

1. Alphonso Lingis, *The Community of Those Who Have Nothing in Common* (Bloomington: Indiana University Press, 1994), 173–174. Subsequent references are identified by page numbers in the text.

2. The keen observing of this unreality is for me the most powerful element of Joan Didion's recent memoir of the death of her husband, *The Year of Magical Thinking* (New York: Knopf, 2005).

3. Sigmund Freud, "Mourning and Melancholia," in *Collected Papers, Volume IV*, trans. Joan Riviere (London: Hogarth Press, 1949), 153. Subsequent page references are given in the text.

4. Freud, "Instincts and Their Vicissitudes," in *Collected Papers, Volume IV*, 60–83. This essay was originally published in 1915.

5. Judith Butler, *Precarious Life: The Powers of Mourning and Violence* (New York: Verso, 2004), 20–21.

6. Sigmund Freud, "Thoughts for the Times on War and Death," in *Collected Papers, Volume IV*, 310.

7. Ibid., 311.

8. Butler, *Precarious Life*, 36. Subsequent page references are given in the text.

9. Anne Norton, *Republic of Words* (Chicago: University of Chicago Press, 1996).

10. Judith Butler, *Antigone's Claim: Kinship Between Life and Death* (New York: Columbia University Press, 2000), 82.

11. Ralph Waldo Emerson, *Essays and Lectures* (New York: Library of America, 1983), "Essays: Second Series," "Experience," 473. Subsequent page references are given in the text.

12. See Stanley Cavell, *"This New Yet Unapproachable America": Lectures after Emerson after Wittgenstein* (Albuquerque, N.M.: Living Batch Press, 1989), especially 89.

13. Emerson, *Essays and Lectures,* "Essays: First Series," "Circles," 412.

14. Emerson, *Essays and Lectures,* "The American Scholar," 69.

15. The full sentence is: "I take this evanescence and lubricity of all objects, which lets them slip through our fingers when we clutch hardest, to be the most unhandsome part of our condition."

16. Emerson, "The American Scholar," 62.

17. Emerson, *Essays and Lectures,* "Essays: Second Series," "The Poet," 450.

18. W. E. B. Du Bois, *The Souls of Black Folk,* edited with an introduction by David Blight and Robert Gooding-Williams (Boston: Bedford Books, 1997; originally published, 1903), chap. XI, "Of the Passing of the First Born," 160. Subsequent page references are given in the text.

19. Emerson, "The American Scholar," 68.

20. See Walter Benjamin, "Surrealism: The Last Snapshot of the European Intelligentsia" and "Critique of Violence," in *Reflections,* ed. Peter Demetz (New York: Harcourt, Brace, Jovanovich, 1978).

21. Thomas Pynchon, *The Crying of Lot 49* (New York: Bantam, 1966; Harper Perennial edition, 2006), 85.

22. See Avital Ronell, *Finitude's Score: Essays for the End of the Millennium* (Lincoln: University of Nebraska Press, 1994), especially "Support Our Tropes" and "Activist Supplement, I."

Epilogue

1. Henry David Thoreau, *Walden,* in *The Portable Thoreau,* ed. Carl Bode (New York: Penguin, 1957), 363. All further page references to *Walden* appear in the text.

2. Stanley Cavell, *The Senses of Walden: An Expanded Edition* (San Francisco: North Point Press, 1981), 23; all further page references appear in the text. Cavell's own citations to *Walden* refer to chapter and paragraph number; I have replaced those citations with the page numbers taken from *The Portable Thoreau.*

Index